Cambridge 1

Unit 2
Teacher's Manual

FIFTH EDITION

CAMBRIDGE
UNIVERSITY PRESS

CAMBRIDGE
UNIVERSITY PRESS

University Printing House, Cambridge CB2 8BS, United Kingdom

One Liberty Plaza, 20th Floor, New York, NY 10006, USA

477 Williamstown Road, Port Melbourne, VIC 3207, Australia

4843/24, 2nd Floor, Ansari Road, Daryaganj, Delhi – 110002, India

79 Anson Road, #06–04/06, Singapore 079906

Cambridge University Press is part of the University of Cambridge.

It furthers the University's mission by disseminating knowledge in the pursuit of education, learning and research at the highest international levels of excellence.

Information on this title: education.cambridge.org

The Cambridge Latin Course is an outcome of work jointly commissioned by the Cambridge School Classics Project and the Schools Council © Schools Council 1970, 1982 (succeeded by the School Curriculum Development Committee © SCDC Publications 1988).

First published 1970
Second edition 1982
Third edition 1988
Fourth edition 2001
Fifth edition 2015
20 19 18 17 16 15 14 13 12 11 10 9 8 7 6 5 4

Printed in the United States of America by Edwards Brothers Malloy

Library of Congress Cataloging in Publication Data

Data available

ISBN 978–1–107–65172–2

Contents

PREFACE

It is almost fifty years since the University of Cambridge School Classics Project (CSCP) began to research and develop *"materials and techniques which will accelerate and improve pupils' ability to read classical Latin literature and widen their knowledge of classical civilisation."* This Fifth Edition of the *Cambridge Latin Course* therefore builds on half a century of experience in researching, trialing, developing, and improving what is now the world's leading Latin program.

The *Course* was last revised in the late 1990s and the Fourth Edition has served teachers and students well for many years. A new edition will always present authors and editors with opportunities for development and change. On this occasion, following extensive discussion with teachers, we have chosen to:

- improve the physical layout of the material, increasing the page size to allow new vocabulary to be glossed alongside, rather than below, the reading passages. This layout has been found to improve students' reading fluency as it enables them to find glossed vocabulary more quickly and to return to their place in the reading material more easily;

- shorten the Course very slightly, primarily by gently trimming the reading passages, but also by occasionally removing a whole story, to take account of a slight reduction in teaching time;

- increase female representation within the story line, notably by introducing Lucia, a daughter for Caecilius and Metella. Where appropriate, the cultural material has also been reviewed to reflect recent research on women's lives in the Roman world;

- introduce color into the line drawings. Our aim is to portray more accurately the physical appearance of the Roman world and help students to realize that the ancient world was a world full of color.

Teachers who have used previous editions of the Course will note how heavily the Fifth Edition relies on the work done by earlier authors and editors. The previous work of Clarence Greig, Jill Dalladay, Roger Dalladay, Robin Griffin, David Morton, and Pat Story remains very much at the heart of this edition: most of what you will read, both in the student texts and in the teacher manuals, was originally their creation. Colleagues in the USA and Canada, particularly Martha Altieri, Pat Bell, Sarah Bjorkman, Ginny Blasi, Joe Davenport, Stan Farrow, Donna Gerard, William Lee, Clyde Lehmann, and Mark Pearsall have provided many insights, both into the development of the North American Fourth Edition and into the range of educational environments in which it is now used. It has been a source of great pleasure and learning to observe so many diverse and interesting lessons, from as far afield as Seattle, Boston, and San Antonio, and to talk with students and teachers in classrooms across North America.

Much of the work of the CSCP team takes place in a small attic in Cambridge, often quietly and usually without notice. It therefore gives me particular pleasure to have the opportunity to thank publicly my many colleagues who have together created this Fifth Edition. Ian Colvin, Martin Dawes, Christine Delaney, Bar Roden, Sukey Sleeper, Hannah Smith, Tony Smith, and Laila Tims have all played important roles in the revision process. Dr Maria Kilby deserves a special note of thanks for her careful research, particularly in the areas of color and female representation, her untiring attention to detail, and her very good humor over many years.

Special thanks are due also to Ben Harris, Classics editor at Cambridge University Press, who has gone far beyond the call of duty to deliver this edition, and whose patience and composure appear to know no limit. Few publishers would take the time to visit classrooms across North America, build real friendships with teachers, and understand their needs and their varying situations. Ben has done us a very great service and we are deeply indebted to him.

Finally, we would all like to thank the many teachers and students from around the world whose thoughts, ideas and experiences shape and inspire everything we do.

R. W. Griffiths, Director
Cambridge School Classics Project

SCOPE AND SEQUENCE

Stage	Name	Cultural context	Main language features
13	**in Britanniā**	Mining and farming; life in the Roman empire; the career of Salvius; the life of Rufilla; British tribal system.	Infinitive + **volō**, **nōlō**, **possum**. Conjugations of verbs. **-que**.
14	**apud Salvium**	The Romans in Britain: invasions of Caesar and Claudius; romanization and trade; public buildings and housing.	Infinitive + **difficile**, **necesse**, etc. Agreement of adjectives in case and number. Form of adjectives: 1st, 2nd, and 3rd declensions. Ablative case in prepositional phrases.
15	**rēx Cogidubnus**	The reaction of various Celtic chiefs to the arrival of the Romans: Cogidubnus, Cartimandua, Boudica.	Relative clauses. Imperfect tense of **volō**, **nōlō**, **possum**.
16	**in aulā**	The palace at Fishbourne: layout, decor, gardens.	Pluperfect tense. Relative clauses introduced by **quōs**, **quās**.
17	**Alexandrīa**	Roman Alexandria: growth of the city, trade, key buildings, racial tensions.	Genitive case.
18	**Eutychus et Clēmēns**	Glassmaking in Alexandria; government and economy of Egypt; peasant farmers.	Gender; agreement of adjectives and relative pronouns in gender. Neuter nouns.
19	**Īsis**	The worship of Isis: spring festival, initiation, spread of worship.	**hic** and **ille**. Imperative; **nōlī**, **nōlīte**. Vocative case.
20	**medicus**	Alexandria: medicine, mathematics, astronomy, inventions.	Present participle. **is** and **ea** in genitive, dative, and accusative.

INTRODUCTION

This manual provides guidelines for teaching Stages 13–20 and information about the text and illustrations in the students' book. The aims and principles of the *Cambridge Latin Course*, teaching methods, and the planning of the Course as a whole are explained in the Unit 1 Teacher's Manual.

The content of Unit 2

The reading material is based as far as possible on historical characters and situations in two different parts of the Roman empire in the first century AD. Stages 13–16 are set in southern Britain, and Stages 17–20 in Alexandria. Continuity is provided by Quintus, son of Caecilius, who finds his way to Britain and there tells the story of his travels since his escape from the eruption of Vesuvius.

The characters in the stories are generally more realistic and sophisticated than the simple stereotypes in Unit 1. The increasing complexity of the language makes it easier to convey subtleties of character, motivation, and atmosphere. There are many opportunities for students to go beyond the story line to examine the writer's intentions and to evaluate the evidence provided in the cultural context material and illustrations.

New language features continue to be introduced through model sentences. The students meet many examples of a feature in their reading before it is discussed and analyzed. This experience is an important factor in enabling them to formulate their own rules with the teacher's help, rather than receive ready-made explanations.

Exercises both consolidate and test student recognition and understanding of a feature within the context of complete sentences. The level of difficulty increases toward the end of individual exercises and as the Course proceeds. The stories also provide plentiful material for consolidation and practice of language features.

Each Stage contains suggestions for review of paradigms and language features based on the Language information at the end of Unit 2.

Supplementary exercises on the language and cultural context material are available on the *Cambridge Latin Course* website, www.CambridgeLatinCourse.com.

Consolidation and review activities should not be tackled all at the same time. Plan to use a review exercise at the start or end of several lessons. As in Unit 1, variety of activity and content is essential in every lesson.

The rural Romano-British context of Stages 13–16 and the turbulent cosmopolitan Alexandrian setting of Stages 17–20, separately, contrast each other and, together, contrast the small-town atmosphere of Pompeii in Unit 1. Levels of material comfort, cultural richness, personal freedom, and the general pace of life would have varied sharply between these places as well as between social groups. Ask students which of these places they would have preferred to live in and then invite them to debate their reasons.

Because of the colonial origins of Canada and the United States, North American students are likely to be aware of the influence of Great Britain upon their own history and culture. Since Britain itself was once a province of the Roman empire (AD 43–410), as were the homelands of our Spanish and French forebears, the Roman legacy was transmitted by colonialism to North America.

Course planning

Advice is given in the Unit 1 Teacher's Manual. For those moving quickly, some or all of the following stories and exercises may have to be omitted. They are marked by ** in the Stage commentaries of this manual.

Stage 13	**Salvius fundum īnspicit** (p. 12)	
Stage 14	**Domitilla cubiculum parat II** (p. 27)	
	Quīntus advenit (p. 32)	
Stage 15	**lūdī fūnebrēs I and II** (pp. 51–52)	
Stage 17	**ad templum** (pp. 81–82)	
Stage 18	**Clēmēns tabernārius** (pp. 100–101)	
	Exercise 2 (p. 105)	
Stage 19	**pompa** (pp. 121–122)	
Stage 20	**fortūna crūdēlis** (pp. 138–139)	
	Exercise 3 **Narcissus** (p. 143)	

If a story has to be omitted, it is essential to give the students a summary of its content.

Assessment and feedback are important factors in student motivation and achievement. Detailed advice is given in the Unit 1 Teacher's Manual. Students should also be encouraged to assess their own progress by keeping a record of completed tasks and activities and grades (marks) achieved.

Correlation of Unit 2 with the National Latin Exam

Many American and Canadian high-school students take the Level I National Latin Exam (sponsored by the American Classical League and the National Junior Classical League) in early March of their Latin I school year.

Since Latin I students using the Course will normally have reached the middle of Unit 2 by March (*c.* Stage 18), they will be quite prepared to succeed on the Level I exam.

For further information about the National Latin Exam, back copies, and a syllabus, email nle@umw.edu or write to National Latin Exam, University of Mary Washington, 1301 College Avenue, Fredericksburg, VA 22401.

STAGE 13: in Britanniā

Cultural context
Mining and farming; life in the Roman empire; the career of Salvius; the life of Rufilla; British tribal system.

Story line
The farm manager describes how his master Salvius has been injured while inspecting a mine. Salvius arrives home and vents his anger on his slaves.

Main language features
- infinitives
  e.g. *nōs dē hāc coniūrātiōne audīre volumus.*
- conjugations of verbs
  e.g. *cantāre, vidēre, currere, pūnīre.*

- **volō, nōlō, possum**
  e.g. *ego tē pūnīre possum.*
- **-que**
  e.g. *puerī puellaeque in prīmō ōrdine stābant.*

Sentence patterns
(NOM) + INF + V
e.g. *Volūbilis cēnam optimam coquere potest.*
omission of verb in second of two clauses
e.g. *ūnus est nocēns, cēterī innocentēs.*

Focus of exercises
1 Infinitive + **volō, nōlō, possum.**
2 Nominative singular and plural.
3 Perfect tense: 1st, 2nd, and 3rd person singular.

Opening page (p. 1)

Illustration. Reconstruction of early Romano-British farmstead. To establish the context of Roman Britain, compare this homestead with the colorful town houses in Pompeii and invite students to suggest reasons for the differences; e.g. climate, local materials, remoteness from the center of fashion, agricultural lifestyle. These simple British homesteads are discussed in the cultural context material of Stage 14. Here it is sufficient to note the timber frame, walls of wattle and daub (see p. 39), thatched roof, and entrance protected against the weather. The British costume is also adapted to local conditions. The man wears a dyed homespun tunic, hitched up for ease of movement over trousers, and the woman wears her plaid tunic long over an ankle-length skirt. The mustache is based on the evidence of coins and sculpture (*Poole, Dorset, Upton Heritage Park. Photograph by G. Soffe*).

Model sentences (pp. 2–4)

New language feature. Infinitive with present tense of **volō** and **possum.** Allow students initially to translate **potest** by *is able*, in order to reinforce the infinitive, graduating to *can* by the end of the Stage.

New vocabulary. cūrat (new meaning), **potest, fessus, vult, vōcem, suāvem, agilis, saltāre, geminī, nōlunt.**

First reading. Aim to develop interest in the new characters before examining the language in detail. Establish the fact that Salvius is a wealthy Roman of high status. He is always depicted in his toga praetexta because the purple stripe acts as a useful reminder of his status, even though it is uncertain that this would have been worn outside official occasions. His wife Rufilla is wearing pale makeup and a very elaborate and expensive necklace. The slaves' jobs suggest their nationality and education: Varica, the British but romanized estate overseer, knowledgeable about local conditions; Philus, the educated Greek secretary; Volubilis, whose eyes betray his Egyptian origins; Bregans, the unromanized British laborer; the artistic twins bought by their sophisticated owners to provide home entertainment. While making initial judgments about the background and character of this new household, students regularly comment on the change in tone from Caecilius' household in Unit 1. The illustration for sentence 9 invites such discussion. The drawing of an abacus in Philus' hands (illustration for sentence 4) may intrigue students. It was the ancient precursor of our own calculator. The counting board, with its beads and columns for units, tens, hundreds, etc., may strike students as unsophisticated, but the abacus is still widely and efficiently used in some parts of the world.

Leading questions such as "What is Philus able to do?" and "What does Bregans want to do?" are usually sufficient to lead students through the key new vocabulary and relatively easy new language features.

trēs servī (p. 5)

Story. The slaves' depression is lifted when the farm manager arrives with news that their master has been injured in a plot.

First reading. Elicit by questions the slaves' mood and the reasons for it. If necessary, refer to the drawings on pp. 2–4 to remind students of individual slaves.

Consolidation. Dramatized reading of the story in Latin.

Introduce students to the new format of the vocabulary glosses: *verbs* are now listed as they occur in the story, followed by the infinitive and meaning; *nouns* are also listed as they occur in the story, followed by the nominative singular and meaning. Although you will notice the neuter nominative singular **vīnum** (line 6) and the past participle **vulnerātus** (line 14), do not make any special comment. Students will be given a full explanation of neuter nouns in Stage 18. Treat past participles as adjectives until they are formally discussed in Unit 3.

Further information. With regards to the name of the British tribe, there are manuscripts of Ptolemy's *Geographia* to support both Cantii and Cantici, while the *Ravenna Cosmography* gives Cantiaci.

Illustrations. Slave chains from Cambridgeshire (left) and Anglesey (right), both in Britain. These illustrations make the point that slaves, particularly those working on large rural estates and in the mines, could be cruelly treated, and will serve to introduce the next story, **coniūrātiō**.

coniūrātiō (p. 6)

Story. During his inspection of an iron mine, Salvius orders the death of a sick slave. The slave's son manages to enter Salvius' bedroom and wound him before being killed by the guards. Salvius demands that all the slaves should be put to death as a reprisal, but has to be content with the execution of the guards.

First reading. As an introduction, ask the students to recall from Unit 1 objects found in Pompeii that were made of iron: storage chests, tools, razors, stili, pots and pans, gladiatorial weapons. Britain's reputation for mineral wealth was one of the reasons for the Roman conquest, and it is likely that one of Salvius' duties was to maximize the benefits to the imperial government.

Discussion

1 Read the section on the career of Salvius on p. 18. Establish that he is a much more important figure than any of the characters the students have met so far in the Course. Ask students what they think about Salvius. Would the fact that he may have been subject to pressure from the emperor to maintain and increase the revenues coming from Britain make him a more sympathetic figure?

2 Ask if **coniūrātiō** is a suitable title for the story. Does the title reflect the Roman paranoia about slave rebellions, especially in situations where the slaves were likely to feel desperate?

3 Discuss the rights of slaves and Roman justice. In Britain, at the edge of the empire, Roman officials were largely unsupervised and might be oppressive.

4 Generate suspense by asking how the three slaves would react to the story of Salvius' injury and how they would feel about his imminent homecoming.

Consolidation. Note the switch back to past tenses.

Further information. The treatment of slaves (especially if educated) in the **familia urbāna** was generally much more humane than the treatment and conditions in the **familia rūstica** where slaves were often regarded as animals and worked in chain gangs (see the picture on p. 5). Life for the slaves in the mines was particularly bad. Many died from overwork or flogging. "Death in their eyes is more to be desired than life, because of the magnitude of the hardships they must bear" (Diodorus V.38).

The status and working conditions of slaves varied considerably, from the household where some would have a close relationship with their master, to the estate or mine where they worked in chain gangs under the control of a manager or overseer. The economy of the Roman empire depended on slave labor. Ever since the near-success of the revolt of Celtic, German, and Thracian slaves under Spartacus in 73–71 BC, the Romans lived in constant fear of another uprising, and insubordination was met by the severest penalties.

While it was most certainly illegal at this time to execute a slave without trial before a magistrate, a person of Salvius' authority could perhaps safely ignore the law in a province remote from Rome. What we would regard as cruelty to slaves was not uncommon. Like Salvius in the final story of this Stage, Cato (writing *c.* 160 BC) recommended reducing the rations of sick slaves (*De Agri Cultura* II.4). The mass execution that Salvius initially demanded recalls Tacitus' description of the 400-plus slaves of Pedanius Secundus executed little more than twenty years before (*Annals* XIV.42–45), where treatment of slaves became a matter of public debate, and also recalls the murder of Larcius Macedo by his slaves and the punishment they consequently received (Pliny *Letters* III.14).

Mining and farming (p. 7)

In pre-Roman times the Britons had been increasing their yields and were producing surpluses for local markets. There were further improvements in the Roman period because of the introduction of more efficient iron tools, which meant that more land could be brought into cultivation. The new Roman plow was larger with a longer and broader share. With the addition of a colter to slice the soil ahead of the share, it became even more effective. This change led to the tilling of more acreage than the characteristic small Celtic fields. The Roman roadbuilding program facilitated transportation of agricultural produce while the growth of towns created more markets. Within a short time of the Roman invasion, grain was being exported from Britain.

The main crops grown in the province were cereal grains: barley, oats, rye, and especially wheat. Archaeologists have found seeds of all these crops, accidentally charred and thus preserved in the earth. Most farms seem to have kept animals such as cattle, sheep, goats, pigs, dogs, and horses, in addition to geese and hens. These animals could provide food (meat, milk, and eggs), transport, wool or leather clothing, fertilizer, and bone. Bees were kept to produce honey, which was used to sweeten food. Many fruits and vegetables were grown, including some (like cherries and peas) which had been brought to the province by the Romans. As good iron tools and the new heavier plow became available, the yields of grain increased, encouraged by an expanding market. The villas could not produce everything their owners needed, but homegrown products such as grain, leather, meat, timber, and honey could be traded for shellfish, salt, wine, pottery, and ironware.

Illustrations

- Plow team, 5cm high, 2nd–3rd century AD, found at Magis (Piercebridge), County Durham (*British Museum*). The yoked beasts pull forward a beam jointed just above soil level to a sickle-shaped sole with an iron tip. This the man steers straight with his left hand, pushing it downwards with even pressure into the soil, while goading his oxen forward with his right.
- Relief of lead miner, possibly Roman, holding pick and bucket to transport ore (*Wirksworth Church, Derbyshire*). Mining iron was arduous at every stage. Slave labor was used for extracting the rock from the ground, manhandling the bellows to bring the furnaces to a temperature hot enough to purify the metal, hammering it to consolidate the iron, and transporting the iron pigs. The Roman fleet was responsible for road- and bridgebuilding and engineering of all kinds, including mining. Some small mines were privately owned, and some were leased to private contractors.
- A Romano-British plow reconstructed from wood with the original metal plowshare. It would have been pulled by a team of oxen, as shown in the illustrations top and bottom right. The plow's knife, or colter, would have made a preliminary vertical cut in the soil ahead of the plowshare.
- Reconstruction of villa near Verulamium, with thatched roof and tiled veranda. The lower walls are of stone, the upper of wattle and daub. Notice plowing with a yoke of oxen, cabbages (highly valued by the Romans), chickens, cattle in pen, beehives in wood, timber felling, watering sheep at well.

Bregāns (pp. 8–9)

Story. Varica summons the slaves to parade for inspection. Bregans brings a hunting dog, a gift from King Cogidubnus. On his arrival Salvius is irritated by Bregans' attempts to draw his attention to the dog, and strikes him to the ground. The dog jumps at Salvius, who decides to punish Bregans instead of the dog.

First reading. Read the story aloud in Latin, and let the students explore it in groups before tackling the questions on p. 9 with the whole class. Keep up the pace to sustain interest in the new situation. Students could produce written answers for homework as consolidation of the oral discussion. Where the answer is a matter of opinion (questions 6, 11, and 12), any answer should be accepted which is a sensible interpretation of the situation and supported by reasons.

Sometimes students translate **ancillae dominō nostrō cubiculum parant** (line 8) as *The slave girls are preparing our master's bedroom.* As students have not yet met the genitive, say that this is "nearly, but not quite, right," and remind them of how they translated, e.g., **Metella fīliō dōnum quaerēbat** (in model sentences, Stage 9) or **ego omnibus supplicium poscō** (**coniūrātiō**, line 21).

Consolidation. This story is suitable for acting. It can also form a base, when it has been read and discussed, for grammatical exercises, e.g.:

1   1st and 2nd person of the imperfect (introduced in Stage 12), by substitution for forms of the imperfect appearing in the story. Ask students the meaning of **ambulābat** (line 6), and then substitute with **ambulābās, ambulābāmus**, etc.

Similarly with the perfect, ask for the meaning of **intrāvērunt** (line 18) and then substitute **intrāvistis**, etc.

2   Verbs with no nominative stated, taken in context, e.g.:

vīlicus per ōrdinēs ambulābat; servōs īnspiciēbat et numerābat (lines 5–6).
ubi sunt ancillae? nūllās ancillās videō (line 7).
canis ferōcissimus est; bēstiās optimē agitāre potest (lines 16–17).
Bregantem ferōciter pulsāvit (lines 30–31).
istum canem interficere volō (line 35).

Illustration. Detail of hunting mosaic from Carthage, 5th century AD (*Tunis, Bardo Museum*). The dog is about to seize a hare. The image is reversed for reasons of design.

About the language 1: infinitives (pp. 10–11)

New language feature. Present tense of **volō**, **nōlō**, **possum** used with the infinitive. Differentiation of verb conjugations.

Discussion. In paragraph 4, elicit from the students the comment that the endings of **possum** are the same as the forms of **sum**. In paragraph 6, ask for alternative translations of **possum** and encourage the most natural English version in each case.

Consolidation. Students should learn to recognize and translate the inflections of the three verbs tabulated in paragraph 4. A useful oral exercise is to turn the examples in paragraphs 5 and 6 from singular to plural, or vice versa, and ask for a translation.

After studying the notes and the examples, ask different groups to look back at different stories, picking out and translating sentences containing infinitives. If further practice is necessary, ask the class Latin questions to which they can find the Latin answer in the text, e.g. from **trēs servī** (p. 5):

Q   **quis ad Ītaliam redīre vult?**   A   **Philus ad Ītaliam redīre vult.**
Q   **quid Philus dīcit?**   A   **ego ad Ītaliam redīre volō.**

While the differentiation between conjugations of verbs (paragraph 3) is not of major importance now, it will be a factor in the future. Students will probably enjoy being quizzed informally (during consolidation of stories or in the taking up of exercises) on this point from time to time.

Illustration. Color-coated hunt beaker made near Peterborough, England. The quarry, a hare, is on the reverse. The animals and decorative swirls are made by trailing liquid clay onto the surface of the pot before firing. (*By courtesy of Verulamium Museum, St Albans. Photograph by Jennifer Lowe.*)

****Salvius fundum īnspicit** (p. 12)

Story. Varica conducts Salvius around the farm. Seeing the plowmen idle because the foreman is ill, Salvius wants to deny them food and sell the foreman. He is also annoyed because a new barn has collapsed when charged by a bull in the care of Bregans.

First reading. Divide the story into two or three parts. After reading part of the story aloud in Latin, allow the students time to explore it. Then check their understanding and interpretation with comprehension questions, e.g.:

> What did Salvius want to do?
> Who took him over the farm?
> What did Varica say about the harvest?
> What was stored in the granary?
> What was the name of the slave in charge of the plowmen?
> Why was he absent?
> What was the effect of his absence?
> When Salvius proposed to get rid of him, what did Varica say in his defense?
> Why did Salvius begrudge the plowmen their food?
> What did Salvius see when he approached the site of the granary?
> Why was the building half-ruined?
> Why did Salvius consider Bregans **stultior quam cēterī**?

Discussion

1 *Salvius as an estate owner.* What impression do we receive of his involvement and efficiency? He has a manager, but takes a personal interest in the farm. His approach to slaves would be regarded as normal in Roman society and is based on Cato's advice to a landowner on how to inspect one's farm in company with the overseer (Cato *De Agri Cultura* II).
2 *Varica's character.* Is he the right kind of person to be farm manager?
3 *The conditions of farm slaves.* Why was the life of farm slaves generally much worse than that of domestic slaves? Give examples from the lives of slaves encountered in this Stage and in Unit 1.

Illustration. Wall painting from Trier showing a Gallo-Roman farmhouse consisting of two blocks joined by a colonnade. The master, wearing his hooded traveling cloak (left), arrives home to be greeted by his slaves.

About the language 2: -que (p. 13)

New language feature. Use of **-que** to link words and sentences.

Discussion. Emphasize the unchanging form of **-que**, to avoid future confusion with the relative pronoun. After studying the note, put up sentences on the board for students to rewrite using **-que**, e.g.:

> **Vārica dominum salūtāvit et fundum ostendit.**
> **Salvius agrōs circumspectāvit et arātōrēs quaesīvit.**
> **Salvius ad horreum advēnit et aedificium sēmirutum cōnspexit.**

Consolidation. Oral practice of **-que** linking two words can provide useful vocabulary review.

Practicing the language (pp. 14–15)

Exercise 1. Complete the sentences by selecting an appropriate infinitive.

Exercise 2. Complete the sentences by selecting a correct nominative, singular or plural.

Exercise 3. A short reading passage with gaps, to be completed by selection of a verb in the correct person of the perfect tense. This exercise may be handled orally. Insist that each verb be translated in the context of the sentence as a whole. Encourage students to reorder the words in their translation, to produce the most natural English, e.g.:

> *Because the slave was tired, he …* (lines 1–2)
> *After Salvius entered the bedroom, he …* (line 3).

See Language information, p. 175, for similar examples.

Illustrations. Scenes from rural life: man either milking goat or delivering a kid (p. 14); one man and his dog (p. 15). Details of mosaic from Daphne, suburb of Antioch (modern Antakya), *c.* AD 325 (*Paris, Louvre*).

Cultural context material (pp. 16–21)

Content. Life in the empire; the career of Salvius; his wife Rufilla; Britannia. Study of this material should be integrated with reading and language work, as suggested earlier.

Suggestions for discussion

What percentage of the population of the Roman empire lived in Rome itself? What issues might Rome have faced in trying to govern its empire? What systems of government would students propose for managing the empire? What would be the strengths and weaknesses of those systems?

How different might life have been in the provinces of Britannia and Aegyptus, or Lusitania and Syria? How do the provinces of the Roman empire relate to modern nation-states?

Salvius' career shows that he was successful and ambitious. Do the stories in this Stage reinforce this? Do they reveal other characteristics?

Rufilla was a member of a powerful and influential family. How do students imagine the relationship between her and Salvius? What might her own expectations of her life have been? How might she have felt about moving to Britannia?

What were some of the features of the Celtic civilization before the Roman invasion?

Further information

Life in the empire In AD 80–81 the area marked as Germania was technically a military zone in the province of Belgica. However, within a very few years (possibly AD 83–85) that zone split off to form the provinces of Germania Superior and Germania Inferior.

The map assumes that Judea was a satellite of Syria, but it is possible that it was a small province in its own right.

Salvius' character and career Gaius Salvius Liberalis Nonius Bassus, one of the major characters in Stages 13–16 and in Unit 3, became, at a surprisingly early age, a member of the prestigious Fratres Arvales, who were usually all co-opted from senatorial families of long standing and had close contact with the emperor, who was always a member. Salvius was obviously destined for power. He served as a **lēgātus legiōnis** in Moesia (Bulgaria) with the Fifth Legion Macedonica.

Sometime between AD 78 and 81, the emperor (Vespasian or Titus) appointed Salvius **lēgātus iūridicus** (*law-deputy*) for the province of Britain. Identified as a "circuit judge," Salvius was required by his office to travel around the province and to preside in various towns over court sessions of mostly civil cases. Because the local people still lived under their own traditional laws, a legal expert like Salvius was sometimes needed to determine whether decisions made under native law conflicted with Roman law. Salvius, though he was legally subordinate to the governor, reported directly to the emperor and might easily, in his reports, have misrepresented the governor's policies and his own activities. Agricola, the governor of Britain at the time of our stories, would have been busy securing the northern borders of the province by fighting hostile tribesmen. He would have had little time to spend in the governor's palace in Londinium. Salvius would have had freedom, consequently, to do more or less as he pleased, to travel anywhere in the southern parts of the province, and even to interfere in Cogidubnus' nominally independent management of his own kingdom.

Sometime before AD 87 (perhaps AD 84) Salvius had evidently received a consulship and had returned from Britain to Rome. Having served under all three Flavians, he seems to have fallen out of favor with Domitian and was sent into exile in AD 88. He next appears in the records in AD 100 under the emperor Trajan, defending a provincial governor, Priscus. Pliny, in his account of the case (*Letters* II.11.17), described him as a sharp, businesslike, energetic, and smooth-tongued speaker.

Although Salvius had clearly resumed his legal career in Rome, he evidently did not return to political life. When he was offered the governorship of Asia, he declined for reasons unknown.

Rufilla One interesting example of the social activities enjoyed by Roman women in Britain is the so-called Vindolanda birthday letter. Vindolanda was one of the military forts on Hadrian's Wall, the northern boundary of the province and the empire, built about forty years after Salvius and Rufilla came to Britannia. The letter was composed by Claudia Severa to her friend Sulpicia Lepidina, inviting her to her birthday party. Both women were the wives of military commanders and probably lived in forts along the Wall. A scribe wrote most of the Vindolanda letter, but Claudia Severa wrote the closing lines herself, one of the earliest known examples of writing in Latin by a woman.

Britannia The quotations are from Catullus 11 and Caesar's *Gallic War* V.12. The Caesar passage includes a description of the Celtic inhabitants and some information about geography and mineral resources. Compare Strabo *Geography* IV.5.2 and 4.

Some of the Celtic tribes, influenced by trade from Gaul (modern France), even began minting their own money, although there was no guarantee that such regional tokens would be negotiable between tribes. After the Roman occupation, Rome imposed an international currency for monetary use and for propaganda purposes, promoting the imperial cult. Celtic art decorated bronze, gold, silver, and iron. The stylized patterns are very obvious on their coinage. The Celtic priesthood was the learned class which kept the oral traditions of poetic lore, family history, customary law, and the ritual calendar. They were also the custodians of vision, prophecy, and sacrifice.

Illustrations

p. 18
- The modern Italian town of Urbisaglia derives its name from the ancient Urbs Salvia. The archaeological remains of Urbs Salvia include a large reservoir, theater, sanctuary complex, and amphitheater.
- Bust of Lucius Verus Augustus (emperor, AD 161–169) from a villa in Acqua Traversa near Rome (*New York, Metropolitan Museum of Art*). The emperor was one of the twelve members of the Arval Brotherhood.
- Salvius' career is outlined in this dedicatory inscription in Urbisaglia, once Urbs Salvia (CIL IX, 5533; Dessau, H. *Inscriptiones Latinae Selectae* (Weidmann, 1892–1916), 1011):
  GAIO SALVIO, GAII FILIO, VELIA, LIBERALI NONIO BASSO, CONSULI, PROCONSULI PROVINCIAE MACEDONIAE, LEGATO AUGUSTORUM, IURIDICO BRITANNIAE, LEGATO LEGIONIS V MACEDONICAE, FRATRI ARVALI, ALLECTO AB DIVO VESPASIANO ET DIVO TITO INTER TRIBUNICIOS, AB ISDEM ALLECTO INTER PRAETORIOS, QUINQUENNALI IIII, PATRONO COLONIAE. HIC SORTE PROCONSUL FACTUS PROVINCIAE ASIAE SE EXCUSAVIT.

p. 19
- The funerary inscription in Urbisaglia of Rufilla (Dessau 1012):
  VITELLIAE GAII FILIAE RUFILLAE GAII SALVI LIBERALIS CONSULIS, FLAMINI SALUTIS AUG., MATRI OPTUMAE, GAIUS SALVIUS VITELLIANUS VIVOS.
- Statue of Livia Drusilla, wife of the Emperor Augustus, dressed as a priestess (*Naples, Archaeological Museum*).
- The remains of the temple dedicated to the goddess Salus Augusta in Urbisaglia. Salus Augusta protected the emperor, and the temple was probably used for the imperial cult.

p. 20
- Reconstructed roundhouses, Butser Experimental Ancient Farm, Hampshire, England.
- Bronze horse harness mount (3 in or 79 mm) from East Anglia, with red enamel decoration and swirling abstract patterns typical of Celtic taste (*photograph courtesy of University of Cambridge Museum of Archaeology and Anthropology*).
- Celtic coin (*Institute of Archaeology, University of Oxford*).

p. 21
- Since students will likely know little of British geography, use this map (or any other suitable equivalent) to remind them of the settings for stories or cultural context notes.
- Coin minted in Camulodunum by Cunobelin, king of the Catuvellauni (d. AD 41), with CVN and horse on other side (*British Museum*). Under Claudius the Romans took over his tribal stronghold at Colchester as their first provincial capital, later transferring to London.
- Reconstruction of burial of Briton, late 1st century BC, Hertfordshire, England (*British Museum*). It contained a Roman silver wine-cup, evidence of trade after Caesar's invasion but before the Claudian settlement.

p. 22
Rich torques like this were commonly worn into battle by warrior chieftains. They illustrate the high level of Celtic craftsmanship and the emphasis placed on portable wealth and symbols of status. This was one of twelve *c.* 70 BC found in Norfolk, England (*British Museum*).

Suggestions for further activities

1   Compare the map of the Roman empire (pp. 16–17) with a political map of modern Europe, North Africa, and the Middle East. Prepare a presentation on the similarities and differences between the Roman provinces and the location of the modern nation-states.

2   Write a diary entry for a day in the life of either Salvius or Rufilla, including what you have done during the day and also your longer-term aspirations.

3   Write a story about a slave transferred from a farm to a mine, or a group play about slaves' everyday life in a British villa.

4   Create a presentation on Roman farming, using appropriate slides of your own farm complemented by slides of your own drawings of other aspects of Roman farming.

5   Investigate Celtic society before the arrival of the Romans. Take one artifact (for example, the bronze and enamel ornament from a horse harness on p. 20) and investigate how it was made and therefore what professions and skills would have been necessary to make it. For example, what professions and skills would be necessary to turn the metal from an ore in the ground to the artistic form you see? What picture can you build up of Celtic society from this one artifact?

Vocabulary checklist (p. 22)

Discuss the format used in the Vocabulary checklists from now on. *Verbs*: 1st person singular, present tense (met in Stage 4), present infinitive (met in Stage 13), 1st person singular, perfect tense (met in Stage 12). *Nouns*: 1st, 2nd, and 3rd declension nouns are listed by their nominative singular form (the genitive is added in Stage 17).

aedificium is from the Latin verb aedificāre, which in turn comes from the words aedēs meaning "building" and facere, "to make."

nōlō [nē + volō] is the negative of volō.

nūllus is a combination of nē meaning "not" and ūllus, "any."

Phrases for discussion

Each of the following famous Latin phrases contains vocabulary from the current Vocabulary checklist. For additional information on each phrase, consult Ehrlich, *Amo, Amas, Amat and More* or other books of this type.

> nil sine magno labore vita dedit mortalibus [vīta]
> unus vir, nullus vir [nūllus] (two heads are better than one)
> per se
> novus homo

STAGE 14: apud Salvium

Cultural context
The Romans in Britain: invasions of Caesar and Claudius; romanization and trade; public buildings and housing.

Story line
Salvius and Rufilla quarrel over their country estate. The maid gets the cook to do her housework. Rufilla uses Salvius' best furnishings to decorate a room for her relative, Quintus. Invited to visit King Cogidubnus, Salvius searches in vain for a gift as splendid as Quintus'.

Main language features
- infinitive + **difficile**, **necesse**, etc.
  e.g. *difficile est mihi amīcās relinquere.*
- agreement of adjectives in case and number
  e.g. *amphorae gravēs sunt.*
- prepositional phrases
  e.g. *Quīntus ad vīllam advēnit. Salvius ē vīllā contendit.*
- ablative singular and plural
  e.g. *haec vīlla ab urbe longē abest. Salvius dē urbe Pompēīs quaerēbat.*

Sentence patterns
decorum, etc. + **est** + DAT + (ACC) + INF
e.g. *difficile est mihi magnam amphoram portāre.*

Focus of exercises
1. Agreement of adjectives.
2. Imperfect tense of **sum**.

Opening page (p. 23)

apud here has a slightly different meaning from the one they met in Stage 13, "among," in the phrase **apud Canticōs**. If the students know some French, encourage them to draw an analogy between **apud** and French *chez* as in *chez Sylvie, chez moi.*

Illustration. Reconstruction of Romano-British room (*Museum of London*), since remodeled. The pottery is authentic, and the cupboard is based on a relief showing items for use by the dead in the next world, from inside a Romano-German sarcophagus. Red and black decor was high-status decoration in Herculaneum, so the room aspires to Roman elegance even in Britain. Reserve discussion of the picture until **Rūfilla** (p. 25) is read.

Model sentences (p. 24)

New language features. Subjective infinitive with **difficile est** and **necesse est**. This extension of the use of the infinitive causes few problems and will not be outlined in a formal About the language note.

Imperative plural. The singular was introduced in Stage 10. The language note on the imperative does not occur until Stage 19, p. 123. Comment at this stage is generally unnecessary since the context makes the meaning absolutely clear.

New vocabulary. amphorae, plaustrō, gravis, prō, necesse.

First reading. The translation is usually straightforward. If students experience difficulty with any of the features, give them additional examples.

Discussion. Varica's difficulty in establishing his authority with his fellow slaves. His fellow-Briton, Bregans, is left to bear the brunt of his orders, not without complaint. Students with older siblings may show some sympathy for Bregans.

Consolidation. Reread dramatically in groups of four to establish as a unit the infinitive + **difficile** and **necesse est**.

Rūfilla (p. 25)

Story. Rufilla complains of her life on a country estate in winter, far from London and her friends. Salvius reminds her that she chose the house herself and has the benefits of a large household.

First reading. Set the scene by studying the illustration on p. 23. After a lively Latin reading, groups could be asked to prepare the speeches of Rufilla or Salvius for dramatic reading, initially in English, then in Latin.

Discussion

1 *Rufilla* should not be casually dismissed as a nagging wife. Her name Vitellia suggests that she came from an old family of the Roman nobility, probably with a number of country estates in the most beautiful parts of Italy as well as a town house in Rome. As the wife of Salvius she would have been courted as a central figure in society when she arrived in London. Nevertheless, she would have felt comparatively isolated away from the warmer social (and meteorological) climate in Rome.

2 *Domestic slaves.* The number, tasks, and status of the various slaves can be noted from this and following stories. Ask the students why Rufilla sent her **ōrnātrīcēs** from the room before arguing with Salvius.

3 *London* was probably by this time, about AD 80 or 81, the administrative center of Britain. By making his base in London, Salvius would have had good communications with Rome and other parts of Britain, as well as access to imported luxuries.

Consolidation. This is a useful story for reviewing verbs, in different tenses and persons, in context.

Illustration. Ornate comb, probably made of bone, likely to have belonged to a wealthy, fashionable woman; and manicure set including nail cleaners, cosmetic scoops, and (at right) tweezers (*Museum of London*).

Note. There are minor differences between this story and the video dramatization.

Domitilla cubiculum parat I (pp. 26–27)

Story. Domitilla, a hairdresser, resents being ordered to sweep the guest bedroom. Her tears prompt the cook to do it for her, and she rewards him with a kiss.

First reading. Take the story quickly, perhaps leading the class through it with comprehension questions, inviting more precise translation of verbs or sentences which you wish them to notice, e.g.:

> **necesse est nōbīs cubiculum parāre** (line 3).
> **necesse est tibi cubiculum verrere** (line 7).
> **cubiculum verrere nōlēbat** (line 10).
> **nōn decōrum est ōrnātrīcibus cubiculum verrere** (lines 11–12).
> **necesse est mihi cubiculum parāre** (lines 17–18).
> **nōn diūtius labōrāre possum** (line 18).

Treat **nōlī lacrimāre** as a vocabulary item at this point. More examples will be introduced before the discussion in Stage 19.

Consolidation. This story is suitable for illustrations by students or teacher.

Illustration. Decoration on a family tomb in Germany illustrating the distribution of tasks between the **ōrnātrīcēs** who were responsible for dressing and making up their mistress: front hair, back hair, holding the mirror, holding a jug. Basketwork chairs were popular with Roman ladies (*Trier, Landesmuseum*).

Domitilla cubiculum parat II (p. 27)

Story. Domitilla gets the old slave woman Marcia to wash the floor, then hurries to her mistress to gain credit. Rufilla praises the cleaning but laments the plainness of the room. Domitilla helpfully or mischievously reminds her of the luxurious furniture in Salvius' study.

First reading. Students may still need help to translate in a natural English order those sentences with embedded subordinate clauses, e.g.:

> **Domitilla, ubi … clāmāvit** (lines 2–3).
> **Marcia, quamquam … dīxit** (line 6).
> **sed, quamquam … dormīre** (lines 12–14).

Discussion. Note the irony of the title. Students may also be encouraged to comment on Domitilla's status as an **ōrnātrīx**, her character, and her relationship with Marcia, Volubilis, and Rufilla.

Consolidation. This story lends itself to oral practice of phrases containing the infinitive.

About the language 1: adjectives (pp. 28–29)

New language feature. Adjectives: function, agreement (case and number), and position. Adjectives are introduced step by step. The later steps, which should not be anticipated, are:

> agreement of adjectives of a different declension from the noun (p. 31);
> agreement of adjectives by gender (Stage 18, p. 98).

Discussion. In paragraphs 3 and 5, if students are having difficulty with the technical terms, help them to approach the pairing by asking questions about the meaning: *Who* was frightened? *Who* was good? *Who* were happy?

Consolidation. It is a good idea to return to this note briefly in several consecutive lessons, asking the students to translate and explain the examples, so that these become sufficiently familiar to be a point of reference if difficulties arise later. If, for further practice, you ask students to find noun–adjective pairs in previous or current stories, restrict the choice to those of the same declension.

Illustration. Guilloche border to mosaic floor, very common in Roman Britain (*Fishbourne Palace*).

in tablīnō (p. 30)

Story. Rufilla finds Salvius annoyed about his missing furniture, especially as Quintus, now revealed as the unexpected guest, comes from Pompeii, whose citizens Salvius mistreats.

First reading. Students will already be anticipating Salvius' displeasure and, in turn, will be pleasantly surprised to meet Quintus again; therefore, the interest level should be easy to maintain. Possible comprehension questions include:

What does Salvius have to do?

Why does Rufilla address him as **mī Salvī** and **mī cārissime**?

What mood is Salvius in? Why?

Why is Salvius not able to find his chair and cupboard? What else is missing from the study?

Why is Rufilla pleased about Quintus' visit? Why does Salvius not like the idea?

Discussion. Allow the answers to lead into a discussion of motivation and character. Rufilla exaggerates Quintus' social standing in calling him **vir nōbilis** (line 28), since his grandfather was a freedman. Salvius' annoyance betrays him into an outburst of prejudice against profiteering Pompeians. This attitude of Salvius may be attributed to his origins in Picenum, a district well to the northeast of Rome, which had a history of industrial and military power. The lack of sympathy between the north and south of Italy has continued to the present day and reflects in part the different levels of economic development. If the subject is not too controversial, students might discuss similar regional prejudices in North America.

Consolidation. Try a dramatic reading by volunteers or in pairs or rows. First ensure the students have an accurate understanding of the text by reviewing:

1 vocabulary, e.g.: **celeriter, cōnficere, aliquid, nunc, cēpit, dēlēvit, probī, dēcipiēbant,** etc.

2 linguistic features, e.g.: **commodum/decōrum est** + infinitive, **num, volō/nōlō** + infinitive, **mendāciōrēs quam, sellam armāriumque,** etc.

About the language 2: more about adjectives (p. 31)

New language feature. Agreement of adjectives and nouns of different declensions.

Discussion. Work straight through paragraphs 1–3, using the simple language of the students' text, i.e. "the endings do not look the same." If students show anxiety or confusion, point out that they have already handled successfully several examples of adjectives which agree with their nouns although the endings do not look the same, e.g. model sentences 2 and 3, **amphora gravis, amphoram gravem,** etc. Ask the students what case **amphoram** is, and whether it is singular or plural, then ask what case **gravem** is, and whether it is singular or plural. They will soon see that even though the endings may not look the same, the noun and the adjective are the same case and number.

Consolidation. Look back at the previous examples in the stories, and ask the students to identify the noun the adjective is describing, and the case and number of each noun and adjective pair, e.g.:

page 25: **urbs pulcherrima** (line 6), **duās ōrnātrīcēs** (line 23).

page 27: **urnam gravem** (line 2), **familiārī meō** (line 13).

page 30: **mercātōrēs Pompēiānī** (line 25), **familiāris meus** (line 27), **vir nōbilis** (line 28), **familiārem meum** (line 31).

Illustration. Outer surface of wax tablet found in a stream in London, branded with PROC AVG DEDERVNT BRIT PROV, meaning "issued by the imperial procurators [civilian administrators] of Britain" (*British Museum*).

Quīntus advenit (p. 32)

Story. Quintus is greeted politely by Salvius. He compliments Rufilla on the meal and comments on the elegance of his bedroom; Salvius ironically agrees.

First reading. This story should be taken at one reading. If time is short, summarize the story line quickly.

Discussion. Is Salvius' manner hypocritical, or is he showing politeness to a guest, or offering civility to a man with the status of Roman citizen? What can we learn about Rufilla's character from her comments to Quintus?

Consolidation. The comprehension questions could be set for homework, following the class discussion.

Illustration (p. 34). Oysters and other shellfish were a popular delicacy. Shown with Romano-British dish and spoon (*St Albans, Verulamium Museum*).

About the language 3: prepositional phrases (p. 33)

New language features. Prepositions governing the ablative and accusative cases. The ablative case, singular and plural, 1st, 2nd, and 3rd declensions.

Discussion. Because students have been meeting various forms of the ablative case, always in prepositional phrases, since Stage 1, they should have little difficulty with this note. Perceptive students, who notice the similarities to the dative case in the plural, may also go on to suggest that these duplications show a language already on the way to eliminating some, or eventually most, distinctions in case, as has happened in modern English, Spanish, and French.

In paragraph 4 the list of prepositions which govern the accusative case has been limited to those which students have met to date. In a reading course, students do not need to memorize the two lists of prepositions, since the stories will always present the noun in the proper case. Comment only on the preposition **in** (mentioned in the note) and the fact that its English meaning depends on the case of its object in Latin.

Note. The "bare ablative" (with no Latin preposition) does not appear until Stage 28, in preparation for the passive voice, which is introduced in Stages 29 and 30, and the ablative absolute, in Stage 31.

tripodes argenteī (pp. 34–35)

Story. In preparation for a visit to King Cogidubnus, Quintus selects two silver tripods as a gift. Salvius tries to outdo him, but can find nothing better than an antique bronze urn.

First reading. Plan to handle this story quickly, perhaps asking the students to prepare it in advance and checking their understanding with comprehension questions, e.g.:

> Who came into the bedroom to speak to Quintus?
> What message did he bring?
> Who was to be honored that day? Why?
> What gift did Quintus have in his box and for whom was it intended?
> Why do you think Salvius said "no" to his steward's first two suggestions?
> Why did the steward discourage Salvius from taking the **statua aurāta**?
> Suggest a suitable translation for the last sentence.

Do you think Salvius had originally intended to take a present to Cogidubnus? What reasons do you think Quintus had for offering a present to the king?

Consolidation. Divide the class into groups of four; ask them to assign the parts and reread or act the play.

Discussion

1 *Relations with King Cogidubnus.* In recognition of his cooperation, Cogidubnus was allowed to rule his tribe, the Regnenses, as a client king. (This is discussed in detail in Stage 15, pp. 55–56.) As the representative of the emperor, Salvius would be careful to lend Cogidubnus public support and respect, and Cogidubnus would defer to Salvius.

2 *Value of metals.* Cheapest is something made of bronze (**aēneus**), more expensive something made of silver (**argenteus**), most valuable something made of gold (**aureus**). In considering a gold-plated (**aurātus**) present, Salvius would be offering something that appeared good but had relatively little value. Does this shed any light on his character? What might it say about Cogidubnus, the original donor of the statue?

   In high schools and colleges where students are studying chemistry, discussion of these objects might lead to further discussion of the abbreviations for many elements; for example, Fe, Ag, Au.

3 *Imported goods.* Refer to the information about British imports and exports (pp. 20–21).

Illustrations

- Tripods and jug. Tripods were often fitted with a tray or bowl at the top and were frequently used in religious ceremonies to make offerings of food and wine to the gods or to burn incense.

- One of seven cups from the Hockwold treasure, Norfolk, England, 1st century AD (*British Museum*), showing that good-quality Roman silver was in use in Britain at the time of Salvius.

Practicing the language (p. 36)

Exercise 1. Complete the sentences by selecting an adjective to agree with the noun.

Exercise 2. Complete the sentences with the appropriate person of **eram**, which was introduced in Unit 1, Stage 12. Students may need to be reminded of the meaning.

Language information: review

Nouns in 1st, 2nd, and 3rd declensions: draw up and discuss a chart showing the nominative, dative, and accusative, singular and plural, of **puella**, **servus**, **mercātor**, **leō**, and **cīvis**, before asking the students to attempt the examples in paragraphs 5 and 6 on p. 151. The genitive is not introduced until Stage 17 and should not be discussed before then.

Cultural context material (pp. 37–41)

Content. Invasions of Caesar and Claudius; romanization and trade; public building and housing. Against this background the students begin to appreciate Salvius' work and position; the events at Cogidubnus' palace in Stages 15–16; and the wider picture of Roman Britain under Agricola which is developed in Unit 3.

Suggestions for discussion

Break up this long section by reading part of it after **tripodes argenteī**. Suitable questions on pp. 37–40 are:

> What did Caesar's two visits to Britain achieve?
> Why did Emperors Augustus and Caligula not invade Britain?
> Why did Emperor Claudius want to invade Britain?
> How long after Claudius' invasion did Agricola put an end to Scottish resistance to Roman rule? Why might the Romans have found Britain difficult to conquer? By what methods did they achieve success?
> What were the advantages and disadvantages of living within the Roman empire?
> What elements of Roman civilization have survived to our own times?

The chart of important events and dates (p. 41) can be used for quick overview now or later. Use the pictures as a basis for questions, such as:

> Why are the Romans whose portraits appear here particularly important in the history of Britain?
> What message is the coin meant to convey?
> Whom does the sculpture commemorate? Why do you think it was made?

The picture of the model of Fishbourne palace provides a useful preview for the next Stage.

Further information

Romanization of Britain For further information on Caesar's invasion of Britain, see: *Gallic War* IV.20–V.23. For further information on Claudius' invasion, see: Lewis and Reinhold II.112–113 (from Dio Cassius LX.19–22.1). See also Mattingly *An Imperial Possession: Britain in the Roman Empire* and Millett & Revell *The Oxford Handbook of Roman Britain*.

The students may be interested to learn that the Celts probably used women in their fighting forces along with their men. These Celtic tribes put up varying degrees of resistance—as did the later First Nations of North America facing the British and French— to the Latin-speaking Roman invaders. The tribe of Catuvellauni, who lived in the area north of Londinium, was quickly defeated by the Roman army in a decisive battle on the river Medway (in modern Kent), in AD 43. The Caledonii (in the modern Highlands of Scotland), though once defeated in a battle with the Romans at Mons Graupius in AD 84, were never assimilated into the Roman province during its 400-year history.

Southern Celtic tribes had already established trading ties with the romanized Gauls across the English Channel and thereby acquired a taste for some of the comforts of the increasingly powerful Mediterranean culture. The tribal leaders involved in trade would soon have learned not only to speak and read the Latin language, but also to shape Latin letters on wooden tablets or stones. Some of the wealthier noblemen, in order to improve their Latin and to learn Roman customs, would have traveled to Italy. The Roman governors were charged with integrating local communities and customs as smoothly as possible into the Roman pattern of life. Rome extended religious tolerance, provided formal respect was shown to emperor worship and the Olympic triad of Jupiter, Juno, and Minerva. Only in a few major cities were the temples of any size. One of the most impressive temples was that dedicated to the worship of the divine Claudius in Colchester. However, the Romans did detest the sacrificial ceremonies of the Druids and sought to eliminate them from Gaul and Britain.

An efficient road system was top priority in every Roman conquest. Swift movement of the legions was essential during a campaign. After victory, there was still the need to police the new territories and keep forts and urban centers supplied with food and equipment. There were eventually over 6,000 miles of highway in Britannia.

Houses By studying the illustrations here and on p. 7, trace the change from roundhouse to rectangular house to the simple romanized corridor house to the elaborate rich man's villa of the fourth century AD. The Latin word **vīlla** means the residential hub of a rural working community, not a holiday home. Salvius' villa would have been more elaborate than the corridor house, but simpler than those of later centuries. The country estate which the authors in Stages 13–14 have as the site of Salvius' home-away-from-Rome is historical, although there is no proof that it belonged to Salvius. This Roman-style villa was built on a site near the modern village of Angmering-on-Sea, east of Fishbourne. The owner of this estate, as the remains (now re-covered) show, was very wealthy, and he would have had easy access to the Fishbourne palace by the Roman road that underlies much of highway A27. Stress the point that the coming of the Romans probably made little difference to the great majority of peasant farmers, who continued to live in round or simple rectangular houses.

Illustrations

p. 37
- Skull of Iron Age warrior, Deal, Kent, 3rd century BC (*British Museum*), buried with an iron sword, with decorated scabbard and belt fitting; an ornate brooch; and a decorated bronze crown indicating high status.
- Statue head of Julius Caesar (*Naples, Archaeological Museum*).
- Statue head of Claudius wearing an honorary wreath (*Naples, Archaeological Museum*).
- This site, Richborough, may have been the landing place of Claudius' invasion force.
- The inscription from Claudius' arch (CIL 920): One large and three small fragments, found in the same place, are assumed to belong to the same inscription. These pieces have enabled scholars to make the following conjectural reconstruction:
  [ ] = missing part of stone; ( ) = expansion of abbreviation
  TI(BERIO) CLAV[DIO DRVSI F(ILIO) CAI]SARI
  AVGV[STO GERMANI]CO
  PONTIFIC[I MAXIMO TRIB(VNICIA) POTES]TAT(E) XI
  COS(VL) V IM[PERATORI PATRI PA]TRIAI
  SENATVS PO[PVLVSQVE] RO[MANVS Q]VOD
  REGES BRIT[ANNIAE] XI [DEVICTOS SINE]

VLLA IACTV[RA IN DEDITIONEM ACCEPERIT]
GENTESQVE B[ARBARAS TRANS OCEANVM]
PRIMVS IN DICI[ONEM POPVLI ROMANI REDEGERIT]

To the emperor Tiberius Claudius, son of Drusus, Caesar Augustus Germanicus, pontifex maximus, holding tribunician power for the eleventh time, consul for the fifth time, saluted as imperator, father of his country. The senate and people of Rome (set this up), because he received the surrender of eleven British kings, who were defeated without any loss and because he was the first to bring barbarian peoples on the other side of the ocean under Roman rule.

The eleven British kings probably included Cogidubnus (Frere 82ff.) whom the students will meet in Stage 15.

- Gold denarius minted to celebrate the dedication of Claudius' triumphal arch in AD 52, showing the arch with Claudius on horseback, two trophies, and DE BRITANN[IS] (*British Museum*).

p. 38
- Lindow Man, a body found in the peat of Lindow Moss, Cheshire, England (*British Museum*), reconstructed in wax by Richard Neave. A man of fine physique, aged twenty-five, likely to have been of high status because his fingernails were undamaged by manual work. He was sacrificed, according to Celtic ritual, by the triple death (hit on the head, garrotted, throat cut) and thrown in the marsh as a sacrifice to the Celtic gods, possibly to avert the Roman invaders.

- Watling Street passing through Northamptonshire (see map on p. 21).

- Reconstruction of temple of Claudius from Colchester, a **colōnia** of veterans. It was possibly the most imposing building in Britain until destroyed by Boudica. The substructure survives as the foundations of a Norman castle (*Colchester Castle Museum*).

p. 39
- Reconstructed roundhouses and detail of wattle and daub, Butser Experimental Ancient Farm, Hampshire, England.

p. 40
- Inside a roundhouse. Status is demonstrated by well-crafted objects rather than the functional architectural style. The entrance usually faced southeast to make the best of the morning sun and offer protection against cold north winds. Separate rooms for different purposes, e.g. bedrooms, could have been made by hanging leather or cloth between the uprights and the outer wall. The smoke from the fire would serve a useful purpose in smoking joints of meat and keeping down vermin in the thatch. If well-seasoned wood was burned on the hearth the amount of smoke would have been tolerable (*photograph by Simon James*).

- Plan: after *The Book of Roman Villas and the Countryside* by Guy de la Bedoyère (English Heritage, 1993). As shown by the broken line, the roundhouse has not been completely excavated.

- Drawing by Alan Sorrell of Lullingstone Roman villa as it may have appeared in AD 360. At top center is a temple-mausoleum, at top right a round temple. Salvius' villa is imagined as that at Angmering near Worthing (now covered up) which excavation showed to be unusually elaborate for the 1st century, with planning and craftsmanship surpassed only at Fishbourne.

p. 41   The illustrations are all annotated elsewhere in the text. Left: Claudius (p. 37); right: Julius Caesar (p. 37), aureus of Claudius (p. 37), Boudica (p. 55), Fishbourne Palace (p. 70).

p. 42   Detail from tombstone of Longinus Sdapeze, officer of the 1st squadron of Thracian cavalry from Bulgaria (*Colchester, Castle Museum*). The spiky hair of the victim was possibly stiffened with lime.

Suggestions for further activities

1   Salvius' career shows that he was successful and ambitious. Write a character sketch of Salvius as he appears in the fictional stories in Stages 13 and 14 or write an imaginary dialogue between two friends, one who admires Salvius and one who dislikes Salvius.

2   Write a letter from Rufilla to a friend in Rome, describing her life, her British country villa, and her occasional visits to London.

3   Adopt the persona of a patriotic Roman sent to Britain, inclined to be disgruntled but impressed, in spite of yourself, by the amenities of life found there. Compose a journal or a presentation of your stay in Britain, illustrating the many aspects of life in Britain that reflect the Roman influence.

4   Imagine you are Salvius and have been in Britain for six months. Write your first report to the emperor, selecting topics you think he will find interesting. Possibilities include: the British way of life and attitude to the Romans, agriculture and industries useful to the Romans, the morale of Roman officials and their families sent to the province on duty.

Vocabulary checklist (p. 42)

num, like **nōnne**, is treated as a vocabulary item only and no further explanation is given.

attonitus is the perfect passive participle of **attonō**, **attonāre** meaning "to strike with thunder." Thus **attonitus** comes to mean "stunned, senseless."

cotīdiē is a compound of **quot** + **diēs**.

dīligenter comes from the verb **dīligō**, **dīligere** meaning "to prize, be fond of." If one does something **dīligenter**, one is careful, presumably because one cherishes or prizes highly what one is doing.

Students have seen **x** as the double consonant **cs** previously in words such as **iūdex** and **dūxī**. **rēx** is an example of **x** as the double consonant **gs** (cf. **intellēxī**). The teacher may wish to explain the difference between voiced and unvoiced consonants and review the pronunciation of the Latin **s** to explain the **g**.

Phrases for discussion

dulce et decorum est pro patria mori
semper fidelis [motto of the USMC]
ipso facto
quis custodiet custodes ipsos?
Deo, Regi, Patriae
ditat Deus [motto of Arizona]
Deus vult [motto of the First Crusade]
deus ex machina
delenda est Carthago [Cato the Elder]

STAGE 15: rēx Cogidubnus

Cultural context
The reaction of various Celtic chiefs to the arrival of the Romans: Cogidubnus, Cartimandua, Boudica.

Story line
Annoyed by crowds on the way to the palace, Salvius has two Britons and their cart thrown into the ditch. He and Quintus attend a ceremony and games, held by Cogidubnus, to honor Claudius. The Cantici win all events but the boat race.

Main language features
- relative clauses
  e.g. *vīnum, quod ancillae ferēbant, erat in paterā aureā.*

- imperfect tense of **possum, volō, nōlō**
  e.g. *Belimicus et Canticī nihil facere poterant.*

Incidental language feature
- infinitive + **dēbeō**
  e.g. *quid facere dēbeō?*

Sentence patterns
NOM + REL CL + V
e.g. *senex, quī scēptrum tenēbat, erat rēx Cogidubnus.*
omission of verb in first of two clauses
e.g. *Rēgnēnsēs laetī, Canticī miserī erant.*

Focus of exercises
1 Dative and accusative case.
2 Phrases and verbs with the infinitive.

Opening page (p. 43)

Illustration. Detail from dedicatory inscription of temple to Neptune and Minerva, Chichester, now built into the outside wall of the Assembly Rooms. The full inscription is given on p. 55. Note the excellence and proportion of the lettering, comparable with anything in Rome. In line 3 is part of the king's name. Tacitus called him Cogidubnus; modern scholars make a case for Togidubnus. The illustration is best discussed with the story **caerimōnia** (p. 48) and the cultural context material (pp. 55–57).

Model sentences (pp. 44–45)

New language feature. Relative clauses, introduced by relative pronouns in the nominative and accusative singular (extended to nominative plural in stories).

New vocabulary. scēptrum, diadēma, rēgīna, paterā, lībāvit, agnum, āram, victima, sacerdōs, bālāvit.

First reading. Read sentences aloud in Latin with appropriate pauses and word grouping. Given this help, the students should translate without difficulty, especially if they have met *que* in Spanish and *qui* and *que* in French. In sentences 4–6 some students may try to make the relative clause passive (e.g. *The wine, which was being carried by the slave girls* …). If so, write on the board the clause without the relative pronoun, e.g. **ancillae vīnum ferēbant**, with the students' translation underneath. Then go back to the model sentence and ask for a retranslation.

In sentences 4–6, students may need to discuss animal sacrifice (see notes on **caerimōnia** below) before they can concentrate on the language.

Consolidation. Return briefly to the model sentences in several subsequent lessons. This makes them sufficiently familiar to provide a point of reference later. Postpone discussion until the language note.

Illustrations. The appearance of Cogidubnus, wearing a Roman toga and a Celtic gold circlet of high status, indicates the ambiguity of his position as a client king. The purple color of King Cogidubnus' toga is not solidly grounded in ancient evidence, but takes its origin from Suetonius' description (paraphrased by Servius in *Commentary on the Aeneid* 7.612) of the purple and white toga trabea of the kings (he means the early kings of Rome). Although they are not shown here, it is possible that the native Britons grouped behind Cogidubnus would have worn blue dye or blue tattoos on their bodies or faces (Caesar *Gallic Wars* 5.14; Martial *Epigram* 11.53; Claudian *On the Consulship of Stilicho* 2, *De Bello Gothico*; Solinus *Polyhistoriae* 22). Archaeologists have found equipment that might have been used for body-painting and tattooing (including cosmetic grinders, needles, razors) in Britain. Cogidubnus himself may even have been tattooed as a child.

Cogidubnus' wife, of whom nothing (including her existence) is known, is imagined to be romanized to the extent that she favors white makeup.

ad aulam (pp. 46–47)

Story. Riding in procession with Quintus to the palace, Salvius orders Varica to clear a route through the crowd. When his men force two young Britons and their cart into the ditch, Salvius laughs with satisfaction.

First reading. After reading the first paragraph in Latin, check the students' understanding by asking them to draw the procession as a "frieze" (in their notebooks and/or on the board), with people and objects in correct sequence and labeled in English or Latin.

Then divide the class into five groups, asking each to prepare a translation for the words of one of the characters. When the students go through the whole story, a comparison of the different groups' translations will provoke illuminating discussion of the attitudes revealed by the words. Afterward there could be a dramatic reading by the whole class.

Discussion. Ask the class to identify the ways in which Salvius' rank, wealth, and importance (his **dignitās**) are displayed, e.g. his horse, outriders to clear the way, large retinue, the gifts they bear, his contemptuous attitude to the provincials.

Consolidation. The first paragraphs are useful for reviewing the imperfect tense, e.g.:

> What was the meaning of **agmen ad aulam prōcēdēbat** (line 1)?
> What would **Salvius ad aulam prōcēdēbat** mean?
> And **omnēs prōcēdēbant**?
> And **prōcēdēbam**?
> What was the meaning of **magna turba erat in viā** (lines 7–8)?
> What would **erant in viā** mean?
> And **in viā eramus**?
> What would be the Latin for *I was on the road*?

Refer if necessary to the Language information (pp. 168 and 170).

Illustration. Reconstruction of Cogidubnus' palace from the east (see p. 70), the direction from which Salvius, Quintus, and other visitors would have arrived.

caerimōnia (pp. 48–49)

Story. In a mixed gathering of Britons and Romans, Salvius and Quintus watch as the king makes a sacrifice, and a wax effigy of the Emperor Claudius is placed on a pyre and burnt in a symbolic ceremony which frees an eagle to fly to heaven.

First reading. Set the scene by asking students why Salvius and Quintus have been invited to the palace. This was explained in **tripodes argenteī** (p. 34, lines 6–11).

Read the story aloud in Latin with appropriate pauses and expression, and encourage the shared translation of difficult sentences before the class tackles the comprehension questions, possibly orally in pairs. Written answers could be assigned for homework.

Discussion

1 *Claudius.* Cogidubnus became a **cliēns** of Claudius during or soon after the invasion of Britain in AD 43. Claudius died in AD 54, and this story is set in AD 80 or 81, showing the steadfast loyalty of Cogidubnus to his patron, and the extent to which he is now living in the past. He does not recognize that, with the coming of Salvius, his position and prestige are almost ended.

2 *Sacrificial rituals.* It was a Roman custom to offer food and wine to the dead at their tombs on the anniversary of their birth, to reinvigorate them in the underworld. Important public events were marked by animal sacrifices to win the support of the gods. The animal was first stunned by a blow, then its throat was cut, the blood collected, the internal organs burned on the altar, and the meat cooked and eaten. If the future was in doubt, the priest would read the omens revealed by the condition of the liver.

3 *Aquila.* The eagle was the universal symbol of Roman power. Today it is included on many US government symbols.

4 *Apotheosis.* This scene is based on the ritual for promoting an emperor to divinity after his death (see Herodian *History* IV.2). Since the death of Augustus, the emperor's funeral pyre had a wax image on the top, from which an eagle (in a cage beneath the pyre) was released. The effect was impressive, and the Romans liked magic tricks (cf. Stage 16 model sentences).

Consolidation. A good passage for identifying instances of the perfect tense and practicing manipulation in the same way as suggested for verbs in **ad aulam** (above), in readiness for the introduction of the pluperfect tense in the next Stage.

Illustration. A funeral pyre was rectangular, with the logs piled alternate ways, sometimes interwoven with papyrus to facilitate burning.

Note. If some students do not know what a pyre is, find a volunteer in class who can explain, or use the word *pyromaniac* as a clue. Refer to the illustration on p. 49.

About the language 1: relative clauses (p. 50)

New language feature. Relative clauses describing the subject of the sentence.

Discussion. Students should work straight through this note with your help. The aim is to enable them to:

>   recognize a relative clause,
>   identify the noun to which it refers,
>   translate it correctly.

There is no need at this point to analyze the relative pronouns. The immediate priority is to recognize and translate relative clauses correctly.

At some point, put on the board examples of English and Latin sentences containing relative pronouns and let students themselves spot parallels between initial *wh-* in *who*, *which*, *when* and initial **qu-** in **qui**, **quae**, **quem**, etc.

If a student inquires about **quod**, it is sufficient to say that the word has two meanings, *which* and *because*, and the choice is made according to the sense of the sentence. Show how the examples in **ad aulam** (p. 46, lines 5 and 10) are unambiguous.

Consolidation. Return to the model sentences, or one of the earlier stories, and ask each student to find a sentence containing a relative clause, and:

> write out the sentence,
> underline the relative clause,
> circle the noun it describes,
> translate the sentence.

This is a useful exercise for the student to keep and use for future review.

Note. The note on relative pronouns in the Language information section (p. 167) uses the term "antecedent" for the noun described by the clause. If you wish to introduce that term in your teaching of Stage 15, first ensure that the students are comfortable translating relative clauses.

****lūdī fūnebrēs I and II** (pp. 51–52)

Story. Cogidubnus leads his guests to the shore for the funeral games. The Cantici excel in the athletic contests, but in the boat race they are wrecked through the over-confidence of their captain, while the Regnenses return safely.

First reading. This story contains many new words and unfamiliar concepts and will need careful planning. The excitement of the competition requires a rapid pace. Try one of two approaches.

Option 1. In Part I, use comprehension questions to establish the background situation in the first two paragraphs. Then divide the class into two "tribal" teams, asking students to identify the color of their boat, the name of their helmsman, and his personality. Once the race begins, each team can translate (and shout?) its encouragement.

During the "commercial break" between Parts I and II, the teams may wish (in character) to predict the outcome. Then begin Part II, drawing on the board the **lītus**, **mēta**, and (later) **scopulus**, as they appear in the story. Ask one representative from each team to plot his or her team's progress (in appropriately colored marker) as the class translates or answers questions on the remainder of the story. You may have to show some diplomacy in deciding which team should draw Belimicus clinging to the rock.

Option 2. Aim to read both parts of the story in one sitting to maintain interest and momentum, keeping control in your own hands and breaking the story down for handling in different ways.

1 **post caerimōniam ... ēmīsit** (lines 1–7): Read aloud and ask comprehension questions.
2 **postrēmō ... intentē exspectābant** (lines 8–13): As you read the Latin get a student to tabulate on the board, with the class's help, the names of the tribes, and the captains and their characters. Ask the students to predict the winner and to keep to their affiliation.

3 **subitō tuba ... ad mētam ruēbant** (p. 51, line 13 – p. 52, line 2): As the class give you the meaning, ask another student to draw a simple plan of the situation on the board, showing the shore and the rock. Emphasize the incompleteness of the imperfect **ruēbant**, heightening the suspense.

4 **nāvis Rēgnēnsis ... mētae appropinquāvērunt** (lines 2–14): Read the Latin aloud sentence by sentence to keep up the pace, asking comprehension questions as you go. Invite volunteers from the appropriate team to translate or summarize the speeches. A representative could plot the movement of each group's boat on the board. Encourage the two groups to become involved, cheering and groaning as appropriate.

5 **Belimicus, quī ... summersa erat** (lines 14–18): Ask the class to close their books and listen. Read the Latin aloud and pause at the end of each sentence to ask for a translation. Repeat if necessary with appropriate questions to help the class arrive at the meaning.

6 **intereā ... Canticī miserī erant** (lines 19–22): Class translation. Ask the students which they consider the key word in this passage. Suggestions may include **cūrā**, **incolumis**, **pervēnit**, **laetī**. Any choice is acceptable as long as it is supported by sound reasons. Ascertain the majority view.

7 **tum omnēs ... auxilium postulābat** (line 22–end): Ask the class what the last four lines add to the story, and let them work out the meaning in pairs. Some may consider the story would be stronger if the Cantici were left in suspense, others may be sensitive to the comic effect, while others may point out the moral.

Discussion

1 *Funeral games* were a respectful but cheerful event in memory of the dead (in this case Emperor Claudius). This story is based on the funeral games for Anchises (Virgil *Aeneid* V.114–285). Cogidubnus' games also have a political function, to bring together the tribes he dominates, and demonstrate their allegiance to him and to Rome.

2 *The Celtic chieftains' behavior* is worthy of note. Previous generations would have satisfied their touchy sense of personal honor in intertribal warfare.

Consolidation

1 It is unnecessary to reread the whole of the story. Select a short passage, e.g. the first two paragraphs or the third paragraph, for the students to study in detail, possibly in pairs or groups, in order to produce a good translation.

2 Ask students to look through the story again, collecting examples of superlative adjectives, or relative clauses, which you could use for oral review.

3 Focus on words or phrases which review a point of language or are important and difficult to remember, and ask students to translate in context, e.g.:

Page 51
> **ibi** (line 1), **postrēmō** (line 8).
> **aliae** (line 3), **cēterōs** (line 6), **alterī** (line 10).
> **aderant** (line 2), **praeerat** (line 9).

Page 52
> **procul** (line 1), **mox** (line 13), **intereā** (line 19), **tum** (line 22).
> **prior** (line 3), **fortiōrēs** (line 12).
> **perīculōsum est ... navigāre** (lines 5–6), **necesse est ... vītāre** (lines 6–7), **facile est ... vincere** (line 11), **difficile erat ... vidēre** (lines 22–23).

4 Ask students to film or write a sports commentary on the boat race.

About the language 2: imperfect tense of *possum*, etc. (p. 53)

New language feature. Imperfect tense of **possum**, **volō**, and **nōlō**.

Discussion. Let the students use *was able* initially, to help them recognize the need for an infinitive to complete the sense of the verb, but they should become confident in using *could* by the end of paragraph 6. Compare the endings of **poteram** with those of **eram**.

Consolidation. List the personal endings **-m**, **-s**, **-t**, etc. vertically on the board. Point to an ending and ask the class to chorus the correct English pronoun. Proceed slowly at first, keeping to the regular sequence; then speed up, darting about. Repeat the exercise with endings listed in a scrambled order.

Practicing the language (p. 54)

Exercise 1. Complete the sentences with a noun in the correct case, accusative or dative.

Exercise 2. Translation of short sentences containing an infinitive.

Language information: review

Review of the present tense of **sum**, **possum**, **volō** (p. 170) fits well with the consolidation work on the story **ad aulam** (pp. 46–47) and with About the language 2 (p. 53).

Cultural context material (pp. 55–57)

Content

The contribution of Cogidubnus to the Roman invasion of Britain, and his position as a client king for the Romans. The evidence relating to Cogidubnus is best studied towards the end of the Stage, when students have met in the easier context of the stories some of the ideas that are discussed in greater depth here. The roles of Cartimandua and Boudica are also investigated, although they play no part in the stories in the Stage.

Suggestions for discussion

1 What help may Cogidubnus have given to Claudius or Vespasian in AD 43 to earn the status of client king? What were his responsibilities? How would this special relationship between Cogidubnus and the Romans be viewed by (a) the Romans, (b) his own subjects, and (c) Cogidubnus himself?
2 Discuss with students the limitations of evidence on the life of Cogidubnus as an introduction to historiography and the proper use of historical sources. Speculation is a valuable educational exercise, provided it is based on evidence and the students are conscious that it *is* speculation.
3 Discuss the Romans' fascination with Boudica. The Romans' view of Boudica can provide a useful lens through which to consider the significant restrictions placed on women within Roman society. Were Celtic societies in some ways more advanced than Roman society?

Further information

The evidence for Cogidubnus' life and career depends on only two documentary references:

1   Tacitus *Agricola* 14: quaedam civitates Cogidumno regi donatae (is ad nostram usque memoriam fidissimus mansit), vetere ac iam pridem recepta populi Romani consuetudine, ut haberet instrumenta servitutis et reges.
    Certain territories were given to King Cogidubnus (he remained most loyal right down to our own times) according to an old and long-accepted tradition of the Roman people, using even kings as instruments of slavery.

2   The conjectural reconstruction of a partly illegible and fragmentary dedicatory inscription (RIB 91) from the temple to Neptune and Minerva at Chichester (see illustration, p. 43).

The dedication of the Chichester temple to Minerva, goddess of culture, may indicate the considerable progress of romanization in this client kingdom. (The dedication to Neptune is explained by Chichester's being near the coast of the English Channel.)

Even Cogidubnus' name is uncertain. The Chichester inscription is missing the crucial first letters of the king's name, and "Togi-" is well attested in Celtic names, while "Cogi-" is not. Other options for the name are Cogidumnus or Togidumnus, since the character who appears as Cogidumnus in some manuscripts of Tacitus *Agricola* 14.1.28 and Togidumnus in one, is usually thought to be the Cogidubnus/Togidubnus of the Chichester inscription.

Although exact details about Cogidubnus' career are controversial, it seems clear that he was a tribal leader among the southern Atrebates before the Romans arrived. After AD 43, he became a trusted protégé and client king of the Romans. Claudius may have been rewarding Cogidubnus in return for services rendered during the deployment of Roman military troops.

Cogidubnus was not just a romanized, Latin-speaking Briton. He became a citizen-member of the highest, senatorial class of Romans. Cogidubnus not only became a client king, ruling his Celtic people for the benefit of the Romans, but also seems to have been given a special title, **rēx magnus**, and to have ruled over several tribes that the Roman conquerors had grouped into a single political unit, called the Regnenses or Regni (or Rigni or Regini).

The capital of the Regnenses was Noviomagus, a site now overlaid by the modern city of Chichester, near the southern coast of Britain. Just over a mile west of Chichester, in the village of Fishbourne, a splendid courtyard-centered **aula** was discovered. This may have been built for Cogidubnus by the Romans as a reward for his loyalty. See Stage 16 for further information about the palace at Fishbourne.

For other information on Cogidubnus, see Barrett and Bogaers. For further information on Boudica (variously given as Boudicca, Boudicea, Boadicea), see Dio Cassius LXII.1–12; Tacitus *Annals* XIV.31–37; Webster *Boudica*; Frere 101ff. For further information on Caratacus, see Tacitus *Annals* XII.33–40; Frere 78f; Salway 77–79.

Illustrations

p. 54   Chichester from the west (*air photograph by Atmosphere*). Roman town walls at lower right. The two main streets intersect just beyond the cathedral. The one running up the center veers northeast beyond the site of the east gate (top), and becomes Stane Street, the road to London. Town walls and streets intersecting at right angles are characteristic of towns founded by the Romans.

p. 55   • Boudica and her daughters, sculpted by Thomas Thornycroft, seen as a symbol of the expansion of British power under Queen Victoria.

         • Coin pictures (*Naples, Archaeological Museum*).

p. 56   • Detail of mosaic (*Tunisia, Sousse Museum*): Neptune holding a fishing spear.

         • Discus of lamp (*Trier, Landesmuseum*): Minerva as Pallas Athena, wearing an aegis and carrying a spear and shield.

         • Caratacus' coin shows Hercules on the obverse and an eagle on the reverse, to convey a sense of Caratacus' power.

p. 57   • Samian ware from government store or shop, deliberately smashed before the building was fired by Boudica. The red pottery has burned black in places (*Colchester Castle Museum*).

         • Burnt dates and one plum found with fragments of charred fabric in building destroyed in Boudica's sack of Colchester (*Colchester Castle Museum*).

         • Life-size bronze head of Claudius from river Alde, Saxmundham in Suffolk, England (*British Museum*). The jagged edges show it was torn from a full-length statue.

p. 58   Detail of skeleton from Maiden Castle cemetery (*photograph Dorset County Museum, Dorchester*). The Romans fired volleys of artillery to cover the advance of the legionaries toward the gates, and this defender caught an arrow from a ballista in his spine.

Suggestions for further activities

1   Write an imaginative account of Boudica's soldiers destroying a Roman estate or the diary of a Roman officer sent against her, with observations about the Celtic tribes and how they fight.

2   Draw up an entry on Cogidubnus for *Who's Who in Roman Britain*.

3   Prepare a dialogue in pairs. Imagine you are:

    a) an old Briton of the tribe of the Atrebates who knew Cogidubnus in his early days when he first welcomed the Romans;

    b) the Briton's son, one of the young men whose journey to the palace was delayed by damage to the cart, telling his father his impressions of the events of the day.

4   In pairs, evaluate the information you have about Cogidubnus and make three lists:

    a) the facts you know for *certain*, and the evidence for them;

    b) anything about him you think is *probably* true, with reasons for your opinion;

    c) anything else you think could *possibly* be true, with reasons for your opinion.

    Find another pair who have carried out this task and compare your lists. Do they agree in every respect? If they do not, why do you think this is?

Vocabulary checklist (p. 58)

dēbeō is a compound of **dē** + **habeō** meaning "have from a person," hence "owe."

impediō is from the noun **pēs**. When something is underfoot, or on one's foot, then one is impeded.

prīnceps is a compound of **prīmus** and **capiō**. A **prīnceps**, literally, is one who has taken the first place or position.

sacerdōs is a combination of **sacer** and **dō**. Literally, then, a **sacerdōs** is one who gives sacred things to the gods.

Phrases for discussion

festina lente [attributed to Caesar Augustus]
veni, vidi, vici [attributed to Julius Caesar]
felix (est) qui nihil debet
multos timere debet quem multi timent
labor omnia vincit [Virgil; motto of Oklahoma]

STAGE 16: in aulā

Cultural context
The palace at Fishbourne: layout, decor, gardens.

Story line
Intent on revenge after his humiliation in the boat race, Belimicus plots to use a dancing bear to injure or kill Dumnorix. The plot misfires and the bear attacks the king, who is saved by Quintus' prompt action. Quintus tells Cogidubnus about his travels since leaving Pompeii.

Main language features
- pluperfect tense
  e.g. *in hortō erant multī flōrēs, quōs Cogidubnus ex Ītaliā importāverat.*
- relative clauses introduced by **quōs**, **quās**
  e.g. *in aulā erant multae pictūrae, quās pictor Graecus pīnxerat.*

Sentence patterns
DAT + ACC et ACC + V
e.g. *ursae cibum et aquam dabat.*
relative clause in sentences with expressed subject omitted
e.g. *servum, quī tam fortis et tam fidēlis fuerat, līberāvī.*
increasingly varied position of the relative clause
e.g. *in aulā erant multae pictūrae, quās pictor Graecus pīnxerat.*
ex ōvō, quod servī in mēnsam posuerant, appāruit saltātrīx.

Focus of exercise
1 Pluperfect tense and relative clauses.

Opening page (p. 59)

Entrance to the audience chamber of the palace at Fishbourne, in the center of the west wing (see p. 70 for overview). Deliberately stage-managed to create maximum impact, it was approached from the entrance hall in the east wing across the formal courtyard by a wide gravel path with hedges and lawns on either side. Built AD 75–80, when most Britons lived in roundhouses, it was very new at the time of our stories, approximately AD 80 or 81 (*model and photograph, Fishbourne Roman Palace*).

Model sentences (pp. 60–61)

New language feature. Pluperfect tense, and relative clauses introduced by **quōs** and **quās**.

New vocabulary. fōns, marmoreus, effundēbat, ōvum, saltātrīx, pūmiliōnēs, pilās, iactābant.

First reading. As the pluperfect tense is introduced within relative clauses, the sense usually guides students to the correct translation. Elicit *had* initially. If students say *pictures which a Greek artist painted*, ask, "Were they painted before Quintus' tour of the palace? If so, add a word before 'painted' to make that clear." In the same way, passive renderings such as *painted by a Greek artist* should not be labeled wrong, but students should be guided to rephrase them. It may be advantageous in this Stage to discuss the note and illustrations on the palace and its gardens before reading the model sentences, giving the students a "tour" which anticipates Quintus'. Then students will be better prepared to accept the Italian splendor in a decidedly non-Italian setting. The bizarre entertainment illustrated in sentences 4–6 is based on rich Roman dinner parties such as those described in Petronius *Cena Trimalchionis* 53 ff. and Pliny *Letters* IX.17.

Consolidation. Throughout the Stage the reading passages will provide opportunities for asking students to identify verbs in the pluperfect tense, comparing them with the model sentences, and translating them in context. Postpone any analytical discussion until the language note (p. 66).

Belimicus ultor (p. 62)

Story. Belimicus, mortified by continuing ridicule, plans revenge on Dumnorix. He persuades the German slave in charge of the king's animals to let him handle the bear until he has tamed it, in readiness for a suitable opportunity.

First reading. Direct your comprehension questions toward the characters' emotions, which are the motivation for the action in this story and its sequels, e.g.:

How did Belimicus react to his defeat in the boat race?

Which Latin words and phrases describe his mood?

What was the attitude of the guests toward Belimicus in his misfortune?

Why did the Cantici make fun of their own chieftain?

What might Belimicus have been thinking and feeling while he was training the bear?

What do you think Belimicus plans to do with the bear?

From what you know of Belimicus, do you think he will carry out his plan skillfully and successfully?

Consolidation. Oral practice of the present, perfect, and imperfect tenses could be followed by the selection of a short passage containing a variety of tenses for written translation, e.g. **Belimicus, prīnceps ... cōnsilium callidum cēpit** (lines 1–9).

Illustrations

- Bronze statuette of dwarf holding castanets (*British Museum*).
- Detail from mosaic (*Trier, Landesmuseum*). The bear is leaning on a tree in the mosaic.
- Dancing girl from mosaic (*Trier, Landesmuseum*). What she holds in her hands is obscure. Encourage the students to speculate. Could it be flowers? A percussion instrument?

rēx spectāculum dat I (p. 63)

Story. Belimicus is mocked by Dumnorix when he arrives late for the king's banquet. He watches the entertainment quietly until Salvius asks for the bear.

First reading. After the meaning is clear, probe deeper with the following questions:

Why are Salvius and Quintus near the king?

Why do the Romans, not the Britons, show interest in the wine?

What do you think of Dumnorix's taunts in lines 5–6?

Why does Belimicus make no reply to these taunts?

How do we know that the bear is well known before the story starts?

Which elements in Cogidubnus' hospitality are Roman? Why do you think he has included them?

What do you think will happen if the bear is brought in?

Consolidation. If Part I and Part II are to be read on separate days, students could be asked to write a translation of Part I as homework. Going over this translation next day will provide an introduction to Part II. Otherwise, postpone consolidation until the entire story is completed.

rēx spectāculum dat II (pp. 64–65)

Story. Belimicus challenges Dumnorix to handle the bear. Dumnorix boasts he can overpower the bear, and Belimicus too. In a fury, Belimicus pushes the bear at Dumnorix. Rounding on him, it lashes out. Panic ensues and, as the bear makes for the king's couch, Quintus seizes a spear and kills it.

First reading. Ask the class to follow the story as you read it through in Latin, and tell you of any sentences or phrases that they find difficult, so that you can work at these with them before they tackle the comprehension questions in pairs or individually. It is a good idea to read a third or a half of the story at a time in this way.

Discussion. After the end of this Stage, the main story line is interrupted for four Stages while Quintus describes his travels. It is therefore important at this point to make Cogidubnus' relationship with Salvius so memorable that the students will return to it easily at the start of Unit 3. Topics might include:

1 *Responsibility.* Who is really to blame for the accident? The German slave? Salvius, for requesting that the bear be brought to the banquet? Belimicus? Dumnorix, who provoked Belimicus to the point of desperation? Cogidubnus? Should he have foreseen trouble and put a stop to Dumnorix's provocation?

2 *Reputations.* What word might Salvius have used to describe the incident to Rufilla: accident, farce, riot? What impression do you think Salvius had of Quintus after the incident? Why did Salvius not intervene?

Consolidation. Language features which could be isolated for practice include:

1 Relative clauses and their antecedents (see note on p. 50).

2 Tenses (present, imperfect, perfect) and the infinitive in preparation for the discussion of the pluperfect tense which follows in the next section. Oral practice could be followed by a written translation, e.g.: **rēx servīs … spectāculum dare vīs?"** (lines 1–12).

Illustration. Detail from the Great Hunt mosaic, Roman villa of early 4th century AD, Piazza Armerina, Sicily (from *La Villa Erculia di Piazza Armerina* by G.V. Gentili, Ed. Mediterr., 1959). Animal collectors are loading captured ostriches onto a boat to be transported for the arena. The gangplank can be seen at the bottom. The capture of wild animals in the provinces was big business and included bears and wolves from Britain and Germany, lions from North Africa, elephants from East and central Africa, and crocodiles from the Nile. Most went to the arena but some wealthy Romans kept them in private zoos for show.

About the language: pluperfect tense (p. 66)

New language feature. Pluperfect tense.

Discussion. With a very distinctive ending in Latin and a single English equivalent, the pluperfect presents little difficulty for students. Take paragraphs 1–3 as one unit, to concentrate on recognition and translation. The pluperfect is introduced most naturally as the verb of the relative clause, but a causal clause is used in paragraph 3, example **e**. At this point, ask the students to look back to the model sentences and identify examples of the pluperfect tense and translate them. Then move on to paragraph 4, where students should be led to notice the similarity in stem between the perfect and pluperfect. (Comments such as "The pluperfect starts like the perfect" are quite acceptable.)

Consolidation. Ask the students to find examples of the pluperfect tense in the last story and translate them in context. Turn to the Language information section (p. 168) and compare the perfect and pluperfect tenses. Ask for the meanings of different persons, gradually increasing the speed of questioning. Put on the board a list of jumbled perfect and pluperfect endings, -**erātis**, -**ērunt**, -**ī**, etc. and ask the students to give the person and tense.

Quīntus dē sē (p. 67)

Story. Quintus tells the king how he escaped the eruption of Vesuvius, decided to travel abroad, and spent a few months in Athens before setting sail for Egypt.

First reading. This story should be treated as an introduction to the next Stage and read at one sitting. Be prepared to help with:

> paterne et māter superfuērunt? (lines 3–4).
> ibi servum, quī tam fortis et tam fidēlis fuerat, līberāvī (lines 8–9).
> omnēs vīllās, quās pater in Campāniā possēderat, vēndidī (line 11).
> haec urbs erat pulcherrima, sed cīvēs turbulentī (line 16).

Sentences like the second and third examples above need considerable practice. See the further examples in the **Consolidation** section below.

The following comprehension questions could be used:

> Where did the king have this conversation with Quintus?
> Why do you think the king was so friendly with Quintus?
> Who escaped with Quintus to Naples?
> How did Quintus raise money after the eruption of Vesuvius? (Remind students that not all of Caecilius' property fell victim to Vesuvius.)
> Why did he want to leave Italy?
> Where did he go first? Whom did he see in the forum there?
> Where did he go next? How did he travel? Was the journey long or short?

Discussion. Questions should help students to recall characters and events, e.g.:

> What were the names of Quintus' mother and father?
> What is implied about the fate of Grumio and Melissa?
> What is the name of Quintus' freedman?
> Why is he described as **tam fortis et fidēlis**? (See Stage 12, **ad vīllam** and **fīnis**.)

Students could trace the journey of Quintus and Clemens on a map.

Consolidation. Practice short sentences with no stated nominative, and extend them, e.g.:

cēnam cōnsūmpsērunt.	cēnam, quam parāverāmus, cōnsūmpsērunt.
dominōs audīvimus.	dominōs, simulatque clāmāvērunt, audīvimus.
pecūniam invēnit.	pecūniam, quam āmīserās, invēnit.
mātrem vīdistis?	mātrem, postquam surrēxit, vīdistis?

Illustration. Acropolis, Athens, from southwest (*photograph by John Deakin*). The upper buildings are 5th century BC: Propylaea, gateway to the Acropolis (left); Parthenon, temple of Athena (right). Below is the theater of Herodes Atticus, 2nd century AD.

Practicing the language (p. 68)

Exercise. Complete the verb in the relative clause with the correct pluperfect ending.

Language information: review

Review the pronouns **ego**, **tū**, **nōs**, **vōs**, and **sē** (pp. 163–164).

Cultural context material (pp. 68–73)

Content. The palace of Fishbourne. The picture essays about the layout of the palace (p. 70), the gardens (p. 71), and decor (pp. 72–73) provide a suitable introduction if taken with the model sentences. The complete account may be studied at any time during the Stage.

Suggestions for discussion

1 What is the significance of the palace, in terms of the wealth it demonstrated, the Roman style, and the location?
   a) *Wealth.* Suggest a list of the different kinds of craftsmen who worked on the palace. Where would they have come from? What materials would they use? Where would the money come from for such an elaborate house? Who would design it?
   b) *Style.* Why should the occupant of the palace wish it to be built in Roman style? What would be its impact on the British chieftains? What would Quintus think of it? Do you think there were any disadvantages to living in a house like this in Britain?
   c) *Location.* What were the reasons for the palace being built in this particular place?
2 Who is more important, Salvius or Cogidubnus? Encourage students to weigh the evidence in the stories of Stages 13–16 comparing Cogidubnus' title and visible rank with Salvius' **rōmānitās** and links with the emperor.
3 Examine the mosaics at Fishbourne. Discuss mosaics as luxury furnishings (and compare with later furnishings such as medieval tapestries and modern carpets). Discuss the making of mosaics. The drawing (on p. 43) is based on a black and white mosaic from Stabiae which was discovered in a half-laid state. A layer of mortar has a grid scratched into it, the design is outlined inside the grid in black paint (from the bowl at front), and is covered by the craftsman on the right with mortar from his trowel and chips of black or white stone from his box of prepared tesserae. The figure on the right is based on a relief from Ostia. It shows a craftsman chipping sawn lengths of rock into tesserae.

Further information

The palace at Fishbourne was excavated between 1961 and 1968. It is the view of Barry Cunliffe, the excavator, that the owner of this palace was Cogidubnus, although no direct evidence of Cogidubnus' ownership has yet been found. If the palace of AD 75 was a reward from Vespasian, it may have been in recognition of (a) Cogidubnus' assistance to Vespasian while he was the Roman military commander in charge of the expansion of military presence in AD 43 and (b) Cogidubnus' help in keeping the legions in Britain loyal to Vespasian in his bid for the principate in AD 69.

Two examples may be given of the expert skill lavished upon the palace.

The builders' working area Excavations uncovered a builders' working area spread over six rooms. The whole area was blanketed in white sand from 1 inch to 1 foot (2.5 cm to 30 cm) thick, containing waste pieces of Purbeck marble, red- and buff-colored mudstone from the Mediterranean, gray shale from southeast England, and marble imported from central France, Italy, and Greece. Examination of the waste suggests that the different operations involved—chipping, chiseling, grinding, and sawing—were each performed in a separate part of the area. The products of the workshops included patterned stone pieces of pavements, panels, and moldings for wall veneers, small decorative pieces possibly for inlaying on furniture, and various household utensils like mortars and pestles.

The garden of the great courtyard Here again the work of experts is apparent. They removed over 7,000 cubic yards (5,350 cubic meters) of surface clay and gravel—an immense task even today with modern bulldozers—to level the site. This was then resurfaced with topsoil. Shrubs and bushes, including roses, were planted in deeply dug bedding trenches filled with loam and crushed chalk to counteract the acidity of the soil. The archaeologists have replanted the gardens using these trenches for layout. The whole garden had a formal arrangement reminiscent of the garden of Pliny's villa in Tuscany. It leaves an unmistakable impression of Italy and Roman skill.

Today only a small part of the original palace can be seen by visitors. A modern building protects the remains of the north wing with its beautiful mosaic floors. The audience room at the west side of the palace and the large entrance hall facing it on the east side across the courtyard have been re-covered. Remains of the south wing, which may have contained the king's living quarters with a view of the harbor that was then close by, now lie under highway A27 and a housing development. The scale of the palace, however, was immense; students might want to pace out on their school campus the measurements, to get a sense of how large the palace was. This very elaborate Roman-style palace must have inspired wonder not only in the king's Celtic subjects but also in Roman visitors. In fact, the palace at Fishbourne may have been unparalleled in its size and magnificence anywhere north of the Alps.

Illustrations

p. 68 Detail from the model of the palace at Fishbourne. It is likely that the site at Fishbourne started as a Roman military base.

p. 69 • Detail from the model of the palace at Fishbourne. The bathhouse can be recognized by its barrel vaulting (see Stage 9).

• Fishbourne's hypocaust. The roundhouses of the Celts minimized heat loss and, whereas Roman building style was more comfortable in many ways, considerable effort was required to heat the rooms during British winters.

• Compare this aerial view of the current excavations with the model on p. 70. The comparison shows how much of the palace and gardens remain unexcavated, as the site is now covered by residential buildings and highway A27.

p. 70 Model of palace in its final form as seen from the south (cf. drawing, pp. 46–47). Note the merchant ship moored nearby.

p. 71 The garden flowers would have been grown for use as well as decoration.

• Lily oil was used in a cleansing face cream, and the juice was applied to ulcers and fresh wounds.

• The rose was popular for scenting the soles of the feet and for eye infections which were prevalent among the Romans (see Stage 20).

• Garden replanted with clipped box hedges in alternate semicircles and half-squares. Out of view, a gravel path crosses the top of the lawn and is lined with espalier fruit trees.

• The same stretch of garden during excavation, photographed from opposite end, showing original bedding trenches cut in the gravel. The diagonal trenches are modern drains.

p. 72 • Restored section of wall (top left). The red dado at base, and panels of plain color framed with bright stripes, would contrast well with a black and white mosaic floor. The light blue panel shown here is surrounded by a frame of narrow lines in white, red, dark blue, and yellow. The panels on either side are orange and the same darker blue as the frame.

• Fragment of landscape painting (top center). There are thousands of fragments of painted plaster from Fishbourne, not all in plain colors. This photograph shows the corner of a picture in a yellow frame. A blue-green background (top half) is possibly water with flashes of light. The building consists of four white columns surmounted by a horizontal white architrave, with a triangular gable. Small impressionistic paintings like this are typical of the towns around Vesuvius.

• An example from Stabiae (top right), for comparison, shows a detail from the picture shown in full in Stage 3 (p. 27). Buildings rise up the hillside (right) overlooking the sparkling water of the harbor.

- Fragment of molded stucco frieze (bottom left) from north wing. Two birds with fruit in their beaks stand on either side of vases of fruit topped with three apples. The frieze would have run round the top of the wall.
- A wall decoration, with original fragments of marble (bottom right).

p. 73
- Group of floors (top) from the time of Cogidubnus, worked entirely in black and white mosaic. Both upper examples are from one floor in the north wing of the palace using (right) curved motifs, composed from intersecting circles, to represent stylized flowers, and (left) straight lines to suggest cubes in three-dimensional perspective.
- Another floor from the north wing (center left) shows a classic design of rectangles.
- A floor from the west wing (center right) has the popular meander pattern also known as the Greek key pattern.
- Late 2nd-century floor (below) from north wing, very large and elaborate. The central medallion has Cupid on a dolphin, surrounded by four semicircles with mythical sea creatures, sea horses, and sea panthers. Between the semicircles are urns and corner designs of fluted shells. Typical Romano-British borders have cables, curved triangles, and scrolls of stylized vegetation.

p. 74 Detail from a Flavian mosaic in the west wing, Fishbourne Palace. A stylized tendril is drawn largely in black but with the nodes infilled with red and yellow.

Suggestions for further activities

1 Examine the mosaics on p. 73. Sketch the separate elements which are combined to make these patterns. Choosing from these, design on graph paper your own mosaic.
2 Imagine you are Rufilla on a trip to London and tell your neighbor about a visit you made to Cogidubnus' queen in her recently modernized palace. Remember to give details of the decoration and describe the garden.
3 Compose (and illustrate) a real estate agent's advertisement for Fishbourne Palace.

Vocabulary checklist (p. 74)

cōnsentiō is a compound of **cum** and **sentiō**. Literally, one feels with another, and so one agrees with that person.

nāvigō is a combination of **nāvis** and **agō**. When one sails, one drives a ship.

nōnne, like **num**, is treated as a vocabulary item only and no further explanations are given.

Phrases for discussion

qui tacet, consentit
flos unus non facit hortum
inter alia
summa cum laude
inter pocula
tolle, lege! tolle, lege! [from the writings of Augustine of Hippo]

STAGE 17: Alexandrīa

Cultural context
Roman Alexandria: growth of the city, trade, key buildings, racial tensions.

Story line
Quintus describes what happened during his stay with Barbillus, a wealthy Alexandrian merchant, including a riot near the harbor and a visit to the temple of Serapis.

Main language features
• genitive singular and plural
e.g. *in vīllā Barbillī diū habitābam.*

Sentence patterns
DAT + V
e.g. *puerō respondī.*
increased complexity in subordinate clauses
e.g. *in armāriō erant quīnque fūstēs, quōs Diogenēs extrāxit et nōbīs trādidit.*

Focus of exercises
1 Genitive case.
2 Imperfect and perfect tenses: 1st and 2nd person singular and plural.
3 Present tenses of **volō, possum**.

Opening page (p. 75)

Illustration. Alexandrian bronze coin, important evidence for the appearance of the Pharos, especially the proportions, and the three tiers. From this and other coins, and written sources, it is clear that the tiers were square at the bottom, octagonal in the middle, and circular at the top. Statues of four Tritons stood on the upper corners of the bottom tier, and Zeus on the top. Note windows and an entrance door at lower left (*British Museum*).

Model sentences (pp. 76–77)

Story. Quintus describes to Cogidubnus his first impressions of Alexandria, and his arrival at the opulent house of Barbillus, a business connection of Caecilius.

New language feature. The genitive case is introduced in prepositional phrases.

New vocabulary. īnsula, pharus, fūdī.

First reading. Introduce by oral recapitulation of **Quīntus dē sē** (p. 67), to reinforce the change of location which is illustrated in the line drawings and alluded to in the title (**Quīntus dē Alexandrīā**) given to these sentences. Elicit the fact that Quintus is accompanied by Clemens, his freedman. Students usually translate the genitives without difficulty because they are always preceded by sentences in which both nouns occur, e.g. **Alexandrīa magnum portum habet** leads naturally to **in portū Alexandrīae**. They use the translation *of* readily and, in sentences 4 and 5, some will suggest *Barbillus'*. Accept any correct translation, postponing discussion until the language note (p. 80). Be prepared to give help with 1st person plural verbs in sentence 3, since the pronouns are omitted.

Consolidation. Use the drawings and sentences as a source of information. Some teachers may like to refer to the cultural context material at this point. Possible questions:

Drawing 1. What features do you notice about the city and which would you consider distinctively Egyptian?

Drawing 2. How many different kinds of people and activities can you see?

Drawing 3. Why are Quintus and Clemens unshaven? Why do you think Quintus is making an offering?

Drawing 4. What does the atrium suggest about Barbillus?

Illustrations

p. 76
- Pharos as described above, merchant ships, Cleopatra's Needles on the shoreline near the Caesareum (temple of the Imperial Cult), and temple of Serapis on the hill behind.
- Street scene including man with stubborn donkey, slaves engaged in maintenance work at the entrance to a temple, toga-clad Roman citizens, other men in tunics, a woman carrying an amphora, Roman military patrol, an argument in progress.

p. 77
- Quintus pours a libation on the altar in thanksgiving for a safe arrival. He and Clemens are unshaven, a sign of travel weariness—and probably of little in the way of shaving facilities on board ship.
- The atrium is that of a wealthy man, with elaborate mosaics and wall paintings, impluvium and marble table, vista to study, and garden with statues. The villa is in the Roman style, but shows an oriental preference for richly decorated surfaces.

tumultus I (p. 78)

Story. Quintus sets out to visit Clemens' store near the harbor. Alarmed by the atmosphere in the streets, his slave boy advises him to return, but he carries on.

First reading

in vīllā … maxima erat multitūdō (lines 1–10) presents a familiar street scene and, after your Latin reading, can be allocated to the students to translate in pairs. Help may be needed with the 1st person verbs. Remind students that Quintus is telling his story to Cogidubnus.

tandem ad portum … nōbīs cautē prōcēdere (line 10–end) builds suspense. Translate it with the class as a whole to sustain momentum. Ask which word in the last line is the most significant, so that they notice how **cautē** heightens the suspense.

Consolidation. By listing ominous phrases on the board as they occur (**plūrimī Aegyptiī, nūllōs Graecōs, anxius, viae sunt perīculōsae, Aegyptiī īrātī, Graecī fūgērunt, cautē prōcēdere**), you can help the students to see how the writer builds up the tension. The list could be used again for vocabulary practice at the start of the next lesson.

tumultus II (pp. 78–79)

Story. Quintus and his slave come across an agitator haranguing the crowd of Egyptians and take refuge with a Greek craftsman. His house is attacked and in the riot the boy is killed.

First reading. Prepare the students for this comprehension passage by a lively Latin reading, and some preliminary translation of sentences which you consider cause them difficulty, e.g.: **puer Aegyptius … dūxit** (lines 5–6), **nam in casā … Graecōs vituperābant** (lines 14–15), **nōs Aegyptiīs … paucī** (lines 20–21). Students might then attempt the questions individually or in pairs.

Discussion

1   *The population of Alexandria.* Syrians, Jews, and Egyptians competed vigorously with the Greeks for a share of trade, particularly in the mercantile area round the harbors. Refer to the cultural material for information. The Roman governor relied on military force to maintain public order (cf. drawing 2 in the model sentences).

2   *Motivation.* Why did Quintus ignore the slave boy's advice? Who was responsible for the death of the slave boy? Encourage the students to put forward a range of possible answers, supporting them with evidence from the text.

3   *Racial conflict.* Students might suggest modern parallels for this racial conflict and discuss the characteristics, e.g.: hostility is easily aroused and erupts quickly into violence; it is directed at the nearest available target and affects the innocent. Although students should not exaggerate the racial unrest in Alexandria, it was no doubt a chaotic city. Vigorous and competitive trade was its daily preoccupation; riot was perhaps its daily hazard. Teachers might read Juvenal *Satires* III and Martial XI.96 for racial attitudes in Rome, taking into consideration that both authors are writing satires.

About the language: genitive case (p. 80)

New language feature. The genitive case is explained by means of examples already met in the stories.

Discussion will confirm observations made by the students, with your help, during the study of the model sentences. If students are unsure, ask them to translate one or two of the model sentences again. Encourage them to use the appropriate English for the context, in choosing *of* or the apostrophe. This exercise will also review students' knowledge of the use of the apostrophe in English.

In examining the forms of the genitive, take **cīvium** as it comes, without entering into a discussion of the rule about increasing genitive plurals.

Consolidation. After studying paragraphs 1 and 2, ask students to find and translate phrases incorporating the genitive in the stories on pp. 78–79, before tackling the new examples in paragraph 3.

**ad templum (pp. 81–82)

Story. A bore called Plancus attaches himself to Quintus and Barbillus as they walk to the temple of Serapis. He pesters them with information about the city monuments until silenced by the start of the sacrifice.

First reading. After the wrenching story of the child's death, this story, loosely based on Horace's *Satires* I.9, presents a very different mood. After setting the scene with stage directions, read the play as expressively as possible, checking on class comprehension every few lines. Then assign parts for students to act out the play in groups.

Discussion will be a part of this process, focusing on what the students need in order to present the play in a lively and realistic manner. Topics may include:

1   *Serapis* was the guardian deity of Alexandria, in conjunction with Isis (see note on the illustration on p. 82). Questioning students on what they can deduce about the worship of Serapis and the behavior of the priests will require them to refer to the Latin again. The following points might be elicited:

a) The large statue of the god was placed in the **cella**, or inner sanctuary, of the temple. Only priests and members of the brotherhood of Isis could enter this part of the temple; ordinary persons would have seen the statue only when it was brought out for a religious festival. Notice that Plancus is able to give full details of the god's appearance, presumably to impress upon his audience that he has been inside the **cella**.

b) The performance of the public sacrifice took place outside the temple, not inside. (Contrast for students the position of an altar or communion table inside a modern Christian church.)

c) The public were spectators rather than participants in the religious act.

2 *Barbillus' feelings.* Ask students to find all the ways in which the writer shows what Barbillus is feeling. In acting the part of Barbillus, what gestures or movements might the actor use?

Consolidation. Practice any features which were giving difficulty to the groups as you moved around. The story provides useful examples for reviewing the pluperfect tense. In addition, there are several relative clauses in the story if the class needs review with those. Students could also be asked to find examples of the new genitive case in this story.

Illustrations

p. 81 from left to right:

- Mummy portrait of Artemidorus, encaustic (pigment mixed with heated wax) on wood, AD 100–120, from Hawara (*British Museum*). He wears a white tunic and a wreath applied in gold leaf. Mummies in the Roman period often incorporated a wooden panel with a painted portrait of the dead person. This example combines a Roman style of painting and a Greek inscription with the Egyptian embalming ritual.
- Man of Roman appearance in his fifties or sixties, AD 100–120, from Hawara (*British Museum*).
- Sculptured head from Alexandria, 1st century BC (*British Museum*). Sensitively carved in hard green schist, it shows Greek idealism and the stylized simplicity characteristic of Egyptian work.

p. 82 from left to right:

- Basanite head of Serapis, 2nd century AD (*British Museum*). An amalgam of Zeus, Hades, Asclepius, and Osiris, Serapis was created by the Greek rulers, the Ptolemies, to make Egyptian religion acceptable to the Greeks. He was worshipped with Isis as god of the dead, of healing, and of corn. The grain-measure crown symbolizes his connection with crops and fertility. His popularity, like that of Isis (see Stage 19), became widespread. This head, which had been sculpted in Italy, was found in the Romano-British ruins of a temple of Mithras. The presence of Serapis' image in the temple of another deity, Mithras, well indicates the mutual tolerance of cults that was typical of the time.
- Mummy portrait, encaustic on wood, AD 140–160, from Hawara (*British Museum*). Probably a priest of Serapis because of the three locks of hair on his forehead and the seven-pointed gold star on a silver band.

- Statue of sphinx with granite column 100 feet (30 meters) high, nicknamed Pompey's pillar. The latter was set up in AD 291 beside the temple of Serapis in honor of Diocletian, whose statue stood on top. It is the only monument from ancient Alexandria which has remained standing ever since.

Practicing the language (p. 83)

Exercise 1. Complete the sentences with noun in genitive, singular or plural.

Exercise 2. Complete the sentences with perfect or imperfect tense, 1st and 2nd persons, singular or plural.

Exercise 3. Complete the sentences with the appropriate person of the present tense of **volō** or **possum**; a difficult exercise because the pronouns are omitted, and the return to the present tense requires thought.

Cultural context material (pp. 84–91)

Content. Alexandria, setting for the next four Stages, provides a contrast to Roman Britain. The magnificence of the city, its history and culture, its strategic position where east meets west and the trade routes cross, and its importance to the daily life of Rome itself, produced a ferment of nationalities and a wealth of opportunities.

Suggestions for discussion

1 *The city of Alexandria.* Look at the photograph of the coin on p. 75. Why do you think the Alexandrians chose this image to represent their city? As the son of a banker and businessman, what would Quintus most admire about Alexandria? What would he find striking about the buildings?
2 *Alexandria in the ancient world was unique* in size (population of about a million), cultural richness (a Greek city of learning in Egypt, now part of the Roman empire), economic importance (as a center of trade, grain collection, and glass production), and government (a traditional bureaucracy now under the emperor's personal control).
3 *Contrasts between life in Pompeii, Britain, and Alexandria.* Levels of material comfort, cultural diversity, personal freedom, and the pace of life would vary sharply between these places, as well as between social groups.

Further information

Size, layout, population, commerce, and trade Alexandria was the second most important city of the Roman world. Perhaps a million people lived in an architect-designed city spread over several square miles (kilometers). It had been built up from nothing but a fishing village to be a showpiece of Alexander's empire. In the hands of his Greek successors, the Ptolemies, the city's natural advantages of large, safe harbors on major trade routes were consolidated; the arts and scholarship flourished under royal patronage; Alexandria became a prosperous, international commercial center.

For details about the Museum and intellectual life of the city, see Stage 20.

Alexandria became part of the Roman empire when Cleopatra, the last ruling descendant of Ptolemy, committed suicide rather than march in the triumphal parade of the Roman general Octavian, who later became the Emperor Augustus. During the early part of this period, the Caesareum, a temple which Cleopatra had begun to honor her lover Mark Antony, was completed by Octavian to honor his adoptive father Gaius Julius Caesar and himself. This temple stood near the shore in the center of the Great (Eastern) Harbor. It was outside this temple that Quintus and Clemens, newly arrived in Alexandria from Greece, made their thanksgiving offering. In front of the Caesareum were erected two obelisks which had been brought from ancient Heliopolis by Augustus.

In the southwestern part of the city, in the ancient Egyptian quarter of Alexandria, was built the Serapeum, the temple which Ptolemy III (246–221 BC) dedicated to the worship of Alexandria's patron deity, Serapis. It was the Serapeum to which Quintus and his Alexandrian host Barbillus were walking when they met the loquacious bore, Plancus (**ad templum**). Attached to this temple was the Serapeum Library, the smaller and younger of the two great libraries for which Alexandria was famous.

The city was the focal point of a very wide trade network. See map in students' textbook, p. 87. The purpose of this map is to show the extent of the empire at the time of the stories and to indicate the main movements of goods both within and from outside the empire. Alexandria's importance as a trade center for both new materials and manufactured goods is clear. It was famous for its glassmaking industry and for its papyrus. Silk came from China, pepper from India, and ivory from central Africa. Rome imported far more than it exported; it paid for this with the revenue from its provinces.

The Pharos This was one of the tallest buildings of ancient times. Designed by the architect Sostratis and built in 279 BC, it had a square base, an octagonal section, a circular section, and, at the top, a lantern with a beacon. Hydraulic machinery may have been used to haul fuel the final distance to the top. The working of the mirrors, which may have reflected the sun by day and a fire by night, is still a mystery. A series of earthquakes toppled parts of it around AD 641, but the square base continued to be used as a lighthouse until the fourteenth century, when another earthquake sent it into the sea.

Style and method of government Alexandria served as the administrative capital of Egypt during the Roman period. The administration was autocratic, with power concentrated in the hands of the Greek and Roman communities. A highly developed bureaucracy controlled the life of the Egyptian peasants and villagers, whose work was prescribed to them in detail and whose freedom was severely restricted.

Racial diversity Because the city was located at the crossroads of trade routes, the population became quite cosmopolitan. Chief among the ethnic mix were Greek immigrants and their descendants; they lived largely in the Greek section in the northern part of the city along the Great Harbor. There was also a large population of Jewish immigrants and their descendants; they lived in the northern section of the city to the east of the Greeks. A large group of indigenous Egyptians lived south of the Western Harbor. Tensions existed between the racial groups living in the city. For evidence of anti-Semitism, see Lewis and Reinhold, II.413. Students might compare Alexandria with certain large multiethnic American cities like New York and Los Angeles, where race riots have broken out on occasion, particularly in the hot summers, or Montreal or Quebec in Canada, where certain French Canadians have agitated for separation from the rest of Canada.

Illustrations

pp. 84–85

- View of Alexandria, looking from the sea toward the lake. The Royal Quarter is on the Great Harbor, left of the causeway linking Pharos Island to the mainland. A canal can be seen linking the Western Harbor, right of the causeway, to the Lake Harbor and the Canopic mouth (now silted up) of the Nile delta. The city walls, enclosing a grid pattern of streets, start near the mouth of this canal. From the western gate nearby, the wide Canopus Street runs right across the city. The temple of Serapis in the southwestern quarter of the city is slightly raised, and the temple of Isis Pharia is on the eastern end of Pharos Island not far from the short causeway to the lighthouse (*painting by Jean-Claude Golvin*).

p. 86
- Posthumous head of Alexander the Great, from Alexandria (*British Museum*). Alexander was said by the Romans to be one of the first people to manage his public image. He wanted to emphasize his youthfulness at the time of his conquests (he died at age thirty-two) and selected artists capable of conveying this likeness, which became associated with him as a divinity after his death. This statue shows the attributes described in the literary sources: upward glance, leonine mane of hair, melting look in the eyes.

- For coin, see note on p. 46 of this manual.

- Modern harbor at Alexandria (*photograph by Stéphane Compoint/Corbis Sygma*).

p. 87
- Map of Roman empire, end of 1st century AD, showing principal trade routes and strategic position of Alexandria.

p. 88
- Reconstruction of the Pharos with cutaway showing the spiral ramp used by animals to carry fuel for the fire kept permanently alight at the top. Colossal statues of King Ptolemy and his queen can just be seen to the left of the tower (*painting by Jean-Claude Golvin*).

- Site of Pharos, with 15th-century Fort Qaitbay (*photograph by Stéphane Compoint/Corbis Sygma*).

p. 89
- Left: Cleopatra's Needles, 18th-century print from *Description de l'Égypte* by Cécile, 1798 (*British Museum*). These red granite obelisks (giant stone needles) had been brought from the ancient Egyptian city of Heliopolis, where they had stood for many centuries by the temple of the Egyptian god Amon-Re, proclaiming with hieroglyphs inscribed on the sides the achievements of the Egyptian pharoahs Thotmes III (1490–1436 BC) and Rameses II (1290–1224 BC). They were moved to the Caesareum in Alexandria by Augustus. The erect obelisk is now in New York, the other in London. These two obelisks, now over three thousand years old, are popularly known as "Cleopatra's Needles."

- Right: Cleopatra's Needle, obelisk approximately 21 meters high, on Thames Embankment, London, England.

p. 90
- Head of Medusa from a rich house in Alexandria, first half of 2nd century AD. The room is a dining room: this design is intended to face the doorway; the remaining three sides have a plainer design, which would have been covered by the dining couches. The central medallion, in very small tesserae, was prepared on a terracotta tray and inserted complete.

p. 91 • The marine archaeological project, illustrated in the next three pictures, was prompted by modern harbor works in Alexandria in 1984 and still continues (*photographs by Stéphane Compoint/Corbis Sygma*).

p. 92 • Warships passing in a harbor (*Naples, Archaeological Museum*). Unlike transport vessels, they were powered by rowers for flexibility, speed, and accuracy. That on the left has a battering ram on the front at the level of the water; that on the right has two steering oars projecting on either side of the stern.

Suggestions for further activities

1 Imagine you are the Roman governor of Alexandria, personally accountable to the emperor. Write to the emperor explaining the causes of the riot and reporting on the steps you are taking to prevent a recurrence.

2 You have now seen something of Roman life in Pompeii, Britain, and Alexandria. Write diary entries in which you consider where you would prefer to live and why.

3 Prepare a presentation for the Chamber of Commerce in Alexandria in which you present aspects of life in your city: its population, area, main industries, public facilities, university, local government, and the cultural and religious diversity of its population.

4 For a class project, have one group draw a large-scale plan of Alexandria while other groups prepare three-dimensional scale buildings (with cardboard, Plasticine, play dough, etc.). Assemble the city using the plan on pp. 84–85 in the students' textbook. (Teachers and students can use this as a backdrop to visualize the events in the following Stages.)

Vocabulary checklist (p. 92)

The genitive is now included for each noun. You can use this checklist to illustrate how the genitive confirms the declension to which a noun belongs, by asking for the declension number of **animus**, **āra**, **faber**, and **īnsula**.

invītus meaning "unwilling," **vīta** "life," and **vītō** "avoid" are often confused. The teacher may wish to create extra drill exercises here on these words.

Phrases for discussion

facilis descensus Averno [Virgil]
a mari usque ad mare [motto of Canada]
ab ovo usque ad mala

STAGE 18: Eutychus et Clēmēns

Cultural context

Glassmaking in Alexandria; government and economy of Egypt; peasant farmers.

Story line

Clemens, new owner of a glass shop previously wrecked by thugs, visits the ring-leader and refuses to pay him protection money. His shop is attacked and he confronts the thugs, who are scared away by the sacred cat of Isis.

Main language features

- gender: agreement of adjectives and relative pronouns in gender
  e.g. *ego ipse tabernam, in quā habitō, servāre possum.*
- gender: neuter nouns, singular and plural
  e.g. *Barbillus, quī multa aedificia possidēbat, mihi tabernam obtulit.*

Optional language feature

- 4th and 5th declension nouns
  e.g. *ille impetūs nostrōs diūtius vītāvit.*

Sentence patterns

NOM/ACC + GEN + V
e.g. *officīnam Eutychī intrāvit.*

ACC + V + NOM
e.g. *tabernam tuam dīripiunt Eutychus et latrōnēs.*

ACC + DAT + V
e.g. *hanc tabernam Clēmentī emere volō.*

ACC + NOM + V
e.g. *mox plūrimōs amīcōs Clēmēns habēbat.*
increased complexity of sentence structure by "nesting" of one subordinate clause inside another
e.g. *ubi ā templō, in quō cēnāverat, domum redībat, amīcum cōnspexit accurrentem.*

Focus of exercises

1 Agreement of adjectives in case, number, gender.
2 Complete the complex sentences by selecting a noun or phrase to agree with the main verb.
3 Pluperfect singular and plural. Relative pronouns and antecedents.

Opening page (p. 93)

Fragments of shattered glass symbolize the violence that wrecked Clemens' glass shop and characterized the protection racket described in this Stage. Two glassmaking techniques are illustrated:

1 Wheel-cut glass (*largest fragment*), the technique used in modern cut crystal, was highly skilled and expensive. Outer side of transparent beaker showing huntsman, spear at the ready, wearing a billowing cloak, with part of hunting dog visible to right. 3rd century BC (*Murano, Museo Vetrario*).
2 Mold-blown glass (*next largest*) is much less expensive. Fragment of transparent beaker, decorated with scenes of chariot racing (*Murano, Museo Vetrario*).

Broken glass (called cullet) is an important ingredient in glassmaking. The background shards here are modern, but Roman cullet has been found.

taberna (p. 95)

Story. Quintus wants to buy a shop for Clemens. Hesitantly Barbillus offers him a shop, which had been vandalized and its owner killed by a gang operating a protection racket. Confident of Clemens' toughness and luck, Quintus buys it.

First reading. This story sets the background situation for the narrative which follows in the remaining stories of this Stage. Read one paragraph at a time in Latin, and ask the students to translate, using a different method each time, e.g. oral, written, individual response, work in groups.

Discussion

1 *Clemens' character.* Why does Quintus think Clemens will not suffer the same fate as the old freedman? (Ask students to quote the relevant words from lines 13–14.) Do students agree with Quintus' opinion? Refer to Stage 12, if necessary.

2 *Word order.* The writer uses the final position in the sentence to good effect in this story. **dubitābat** (line 6) signals a surprising switch of mood, **mortuum** (line 10) adds dramatic impact, **trādidī** (line 17) introduces suspense as Quintus seals a contract with unforeseen consequences.

Consolidation. Concentrate on cases, selecting short phrases and asking students to identify the cases of the nouns, or noun-and-adjective pairs, in context. The first paragraph, which contains recent language features, is useful as a test translation.

Illustrations

p. 94 ● Eutychus (left), with his thugs, is confronted by Clemens in a bar.
p. 95 ● Thugs kill the old man who has refused to pay protection money.

in officīnā Eutychī I (p. 96)

Story. When Clemens visits his new shop, he finds it vandalized, and is told to question Eutychus, who is in the biggest workshop, guarded by four huge slaves. Refusing to be overawed, Clemens walks in past the astonished slaves.

First reading. As you read the story aloud in Latin, emphasize the threatening atmosphere. The students' understanding of the narrative can be checked by simple comprehension questions, and their appreciation heightened by more detailed discussion, e.g.:

1 **in viā vitreāriōrum** (line 4). What are the advantages and disadvantages of having all the glass shops in one street?

2 What Latin adjective describes the crowd in line 4? Why was it **ingēns**? Worshipping Isis? Shopping? Looking at the vandalized shop?

3 What was Clemens' reaction to the sight of his shop? How different was it from the reaction of the neighboring shopkeeper?

4 What does Clemens call the slave barring the way? Why?

5 How does Clemens refer to himself in line 18? Why does he say this rather than **mihi**?

Notes

1 **valvās ēvulsās vīdit, tabernam dīreptam** (lines 5–6). Accept the simple translation *He saw the wrenched-off doors, the ransacked shop*, but encourage better alternatives: *He saw the doors (were) wrenched off and the shop ransacked.*

2 **officīnam Eutychī** (line 19). A genitive depending on a nominative or an accusative noun will be extensively practiced in Stage 19. This occurrence causes no difficulty and needs no comment.

3 There are minor differences between this story and the video dramatization.

Consolidation. Now that Clemens is a freedman, he can act on his own initiative. Twice in this story he acts **statim** (lines 2 and 11). Ask the students to go through the story again in groups, making a collection of the phrases or incidents which tell them something about his character. They could then share their findings with the rest of the class.

in officīnā Eutychī II (pp. 96–97)

Story. Clemens is greeted contemptuously by Eutychus, until he reveals his identity. Then he is treated to a tour of the impressive glassworks and offered protection, at a price. Clemens refuses and leaves.

First reading. Read each of the following scenes of the story in Latin, then translate and discuss.

Eutychus in lectō ... nunc mea est (lines 1–7). How do the first four lines indicate the character of Eutychus? Ask students to comment on his personal habits and conversational style. How does Clemens introduce himself?

Eutychus, postquam ... vibrābat (lines 8–11). The tour of the workshop can be taken with the cultural material for this Stage (pp. 106–109) to build up a picture of the glassmaking industry which Clemens has joined. Why does Eutychus show off his thirty slaves to Clemens?

Eutychus, postquam ... exiit (line 12–end). The confrontation between Clemens and Eutychus offers an opportunity to discuss protection rackets, e.g.:
1 What would Clemens be buying for his ten gold pieces?
2 How does that compare with the price of the shop? Find the cost of purchasing a store in your area, and have students calculate the 10 percent annual "fee" that someone like Eutychus would require from the owner.
3 Would you pay it?
4 How would you direct an actor to say Eutychus' lines (e.g. on the surface all sweet reasonableness, but with menace lurking underneath)? What actor could students see in the role?

Consolidation. This passage is useful for class dramatization: a strong dramatic contrast between Clemens and Eutychus, and other students miming the parts of the glassworkers.

Note. There are minor differences between this story and the video dramatization.

Illustrations

- Base from Portland vase (so-called because it was owned by the 3rd Duke of Portland), probably 1st century AD (*British Museum*). The vase had its original base replaced in ancient times with this disk, probably cut from a larger plaque. It shows Paris in his Phrygian cap holding a thoughtful finger to his lips as he judges the charms of Juno, Minerva, and Venus. The cameo technique involves carving away the top layer to show a different colored glass behind.
- Painted glass goblet, Egyptian, 1st century AD (*Musée Guimet, Paris*). This is one of a collection of twenty-five goblets found in Afghanistan, just inside the empire of Alexander the Great. It shows Europa and the bull, with Cupid to the left. Below, a frieze of shields, showing a yellow shield lying over a blue one.

About the language 1: gender (pp. 98–99)

New language feature. Gender is introduced, in the context first of adjectives agreeing with the nouns they describe and then of relative pronouns agreeing with their antecedents.

Discussion. Work through paragraphs 1–4 with the class. Then look at the first page of the Vocabulary (p. 180), showing how 1st and 2nd declension adjectives are listed with the forms for masculine, feminine, and neuter. Reinforce this by asking them which form of **aequus** (fair) they would use to describe a woman, and which form of **antīquus** (ancient) to describe a temple, etc. Further written examples should be set in a familiar context, e.g.:

1 Clēmēns Quīntō grātiās maximās ēgit.
2 in viā vitreāriōrum erat ingēns turba.
3 Clēmēns tabernārium vicīnum rogāvit, "quis hoc fēcit?"
4 Eutychus officīnam maximam habēbat.
5 Clēmēns servōs attonitōs praeteriit.
6 omnēs tabernāriī Eutychō pecūniam dedērunt.
7 "praesidium tuum recūsō," inquit Clēmēns.
8 lībertus fortis exiit.

Consolidation. Paragraph 4 and Practicing the language, exercise 1, provide good initial consolidation. Stories (current or past) provide opportunities, once comprehension has been achieved, for isolating noun–adjective pairs or relative clauses, and identifying the gender of the adjective or pronoun involved.

The following drill (oral or written) may be used at this point or in future lessons. Using the Vocabulary on pages 178–195, find the gender for each of the following nouns:

1 **agricola, ancilla, aula, cēna, epistula, fābula, iānua, poēta**
2 **amīcus, cibus, dominus, fīlius, fundus, gladius, hortus**
3 **aedificium, ātrium, dōnum, forum, horreum, signum, templum**
4 **clāmor, coniūrātiō, custōs, gēns, lītus, mare, mercātor, nāvis, sanguis**

Answers

1 f. except **agricola** and **poēta** (m.)
2 m.
3 n.
4 **clāmor** (m.), **coniūrātiō** (f.), **custōs** (m.), **gēns** (f.), **lītus** (n.), **mare** (n.), **mercātor** (m.), **nāvis** (f.), **sanguis** (m.)

Drill agreement by supplying a basic sentence and changing the antecedent and the clause, e.g.:

1 ubi est agricola (quī, quae, quod) dīligenter labōrābat?
   ubi est ancilla …
   ubi est fīlius …
   ubi est mercātor …
2 ubi est dōnum (quem, quam, quod) quaerēbāmus?
   ubi est fundus …
   ubi est epistula …
   ubi est mare …

You may wish to combine it with a review of the agreement in case and number discussed in Stage 14. The concept of gender, however, is sufficiently straightforward that most students will have little difficulty moving on directly. You can use the bank of nouns in the drill exercise above as the basis for a quick consolidation, e.g.:

ancillam (bonum, bonam, bonum) laudāvimus.

poētam …, dominum …, mercātōrem …, dōnum …

Illustration. Decorative panel from a wall (see note for the illustration on p. 112).

Clēmēns tabernārius (pp. 100–101)

Story. Clemens gains the trust of his neighbors, including the priests of Isis and the temple cat. When the shopkeepers refuse to pay up, Eutychus blames Clemens and arms his thugs.

First reading. Read the story aloud in Latin and give the students time to study it and seek help with problems before they attempt the comprehension questions, so that they gain success and develop confidence from the exercise. Students might then work individually or in groups on the questions.

Consolidation. Ask students what Latin adjective in line 4 of the story might be illustrated in the picture of Clemens' shop (**cōmis**).

Ask students to find the five infinitives in the story (lines 5, 12, 13, 19, and 24) and give their meanings. If they need to review infinitives, refer to pp. 10–11 or p. 168. You might also ask them to identify the conjugation of each of the five verbs.

If students ask for more information about Isis, confirm that she was worshipped for her power to give new life. Postpone a full discussion until Stage 19, where the subject is explored more fully.

Illustrations

p. 100 • Clemens in his shop. Ask "Why do you think the cat is there?" The Egyptians kept cats as pets, and as hunters to protect the granaries, and they venerated them as sacred animals. See the illustrations and text on p. 103.

p. 101 • Marbled glass (left) had colors mixed together to suggest agate, or other semiprecious stones. Glassmaking probably started in imitation of vessels carved from rock crystal and other ornamental stones.

• Small flask (right) is probably mold-blown.

Language information: 4th and 5th declension nouns

Recent Stages have included increasing numbers of 4th and 5th declension nouns. Fourth declension nouns have usually been given in the nominative and accusative singular, and 5th declension nouns in the accusative singular. The **-us**, **-um**, and **-em** endings cause little difficulty for students who are familiar with the 2nd and 3rd declensions.

If students have a firm grasp of the first three declensions, you may now wish to study the 4th and 5th declensions in the Language information section (p. 156). However, if students are still uncertain of the first three declensions, the study of the 4th and 5th declensions should be left until later in the Course (for example, Stages 23–26, where the use of 4th and 5th declension nouns increases).

prō tabernā Clēmentis (pp. 102–103)

Story. As his shop is attacked, Clemens confronts Eutychus and his thugs. They dare not touch him with the temple cat perched on his shoulder, and run away when it assaults Eutychus.

First reading. Take briskly to maintain the momentum of the story to its climax. Read the story aloud in Latin, to help the students recognize subordinate clauses. The long sentence **quondam, ubi … cōnspexit accurrentem** (lines 2–3) contains two subordinate clauses, one "nesting" inside the other. The commas (as well as an expressive Latin reading) will help the students to recognize the boundaries of the clauses.

Discussion

1 What advice did his friend give Clemens in line 6?
What were the reasons for giving this advice (lines 7–8)?

2 Where have we seen the words **valvās ēvulsās, tabernam dīreptam vīdit** (line 11) before? (Refer to **in officīnā Eutychī I**, lines 5–6.) How might Clemens have felt, finding his shop back in its ruined condition after all his efforts? What word in line 10 describes him?

3 How did Eutychus greet Clemens (lines 12–14)? Was Eutychus sincere in saying this? If not, why did he say it?

4 How did Clemens reply? (**summā cum tranquillitāte**, line 17) Why did he do this?

5 What adjective describes Eutychus in line 20? (**īrātissimus**) How has Clemens finally been able to puncture Eutychus' fake bonhomie?

6 What verb is used to describe what Clemens did in line 24? (**cōnstitit**) How do you explain Clemens' confidence? Was it due to his new status as a freedman, or his religious faith (for more on Egyptian religion, see the next Stage), or had life as a slave taught him to stand up for himself?

7 Why was Clemens alone?

8 What is the last thing we hear about Eutychus and his thugs? Do you find their behavior credible?

Consolidation. Refer to Longer sentences I (pp. 175–176) to revise subordinate clauses introduced by **postquam**, **quod**, **quamquam**, and **simulac**.

Illustrations

- The "Gayer-Anderson" cat, *c.* 600 BC (*British Museum*), named after the man who presented it to the museum. The anatomy is remarkably accurate. Made of bronze inlaid with silver, it wears gold rings at ears and nose, and a silver amulet of the eye of Horus around its neck.

- Spell 17 from a papyrus *Book of the Dead*, 1280 BC (*British Museum*). These books were collections of spells, commonly buried with the dead to help them in the next world. The cat was described in one tomb as a form of the sun god Ra, who vanquishes darkness daily and brings prosperity. The cat in the illustration is based on the wild cat, *felis serval.*

About the language 2: neuter nouns (p. 104)

New language feature. Neuter nouns of the 2nd and 3rd declensions.

Discussion. Because students have seen neuter nouns since Stage 1 and have been introduced to the concept of gender earlier in Stage 18, it is left to this note to outline how the declension of neuter nouns differs from that of other nouns. Including the plural completes the list of major case forms for the 1st, 2nd, and 3rd declensions. Students rarely have difficulty with this note but are usually also intrigued to discover "neuter plurals" in English, e.g.: agenda, data, criteria, etc.

Consolidation. Students should find the examples given in paragraph 4 straightforward. They might need help with **d**, because of the interrogative -**ne**.

The first paragraph of **taberna** (p. 95) has some examples of neuter nouns in the nominative and accusative, e.g. **multa aedificia**, **templum**, and **vitrum**. Students could be asked to find these examples, list them as singulars or plurals, and then write them in the alternate singular or plural form.

Other neuter nouns students have met in checklists in this Unit are **dōnum** (14); **mare** (15); **auxilium**, **cōnsilium** (16). In Unit 1 checklists, students saw **vīnum** (3), **signum** (4), **spectāculum** (8), **imperium** (10), **templum** (12).

Practicing the language (p. 105)

Exercise 1. Complete the sentences by selecting an adjective to agree with the noun.

**Exercise 2.* Complete the complex sentences by selecting a noun or phrase to agree with the main verb.

Exercise 3. Complete the sentences by selecting the correct verb for the relative clause. Identify the noun described by the relative clause, and give the gender of the noun and the relative pronoun. Students may have to look up the gender of some nouns.

Language information: review

Review irregular verbs (pp. 170–171), giving special attention to the forms of **ferō**, and translate the examples in paragraph 4. Make up further oral and written exercises if necessary.

Word order has become more varied in this and the previous Stage (see the Linguistic synopsis on p. 84 of this manual). If students are having problems with particular word orders, use appropriate examples from pp. 173–174.

A second look at infinitives (p. 168), and Longer sentences I (pp. 175–176), has already been indicated.

Cultural context material (pp. 106–111)

Content. The section on glassmaking in Alexandria is best taken with **in officīnā Eutychī** (pp. 96–97). The section on Egypt deals with the ruthless control exercised by the bureaucracy over the peasants, the corruption that resulted, and the exploitation of agricultural and manufacturing production for the benefit of the country's rulers. The unchanging nature of the life of the Egyptian people down the centuries, whoever was ruling them, means that illustrative material gathered from different periods is relevant to these stories set in the 1st century AD.

Suggestions for discussion

1 *Modern parallels.* Ask students if they know of protection rackets or instances of bribery in public or private life.

2 *Social unrest in the empire.* Other examples can be found in the New Testament, e.g. the riot of the silversmiths (*Acts* 19.23–41), and the Jewish riot against St Paul (*Acts* 21.27ff.), which is interesting because of the reactions of the Roman commander.

Further information

In the first century AD, the new technology of glassblowing led to an expansion of the glass industry all over the Roman empire, especially in those areas like Gaul, Germany, and Britain where the wood for fueling kilns was plentiful. By the time of our stories when Quintus set Clemens up in business, Alexandria was a hub for the import and export trade in glass.

The Egypto-Roman mummy portraits, dating from the first to the third centuries AD, have been found in various locations in the Nile valley. They are usually referred to as the Fayum (Fayoun) portraits since so many portraits were first found in the Greco-Roman cemeteries in Fayum, a fertile oasis about 80 miles (100 kilometers) south of Cairo. More than 1,000 portraits have been recovered so far and are in many different museums. The popular fashions of Rome were reflected in the depictions of hairstyles, clothing, and jewelry.

Illustrations

p. 106 • Scent bottle, 2nd–1st century BC (*British Museum*). The sand core, bound with clay, was held on the end of a rod which the craftsman revolved, trailing glass onto it in viscous strands of different colors. While still hot, the strands were combed upward to produce the scalloped pattern, and the surface was smoothed (marvered) by rolling on a smooth surface. Handles were added separately.

• Ribbon-glass bowl, 3.4 inches (8.7 cm) high, 1st century BC–1st century AD (*Corning, NY, Corning Museum of Glass*).

p. 107 • Millefiori bowl, 1st century BC–1st century AD (*Corning, NY, Corning Museum of Glass*).

• Cover in the form of a fish. The serving dish that matched this cover was probably used to serve a fish dinner (*Corning, NY, Corning Museum of Glass*).

p. 108 • Drawing of ancient glassworks. The crucible for molten glass is heated with the aid of bellows. The near craftsman is seated on a chair with a special ledge for rolling the blowing iron repeatedly to prevent the "gather" of glass at its end from flopping out of shape while he works on it. Note the variety of tools, metal and wood, for shaping and measuring the glass to conform with the designs drawn on the wall behind him.

• The modern craftsman is shaping glass with tools similar to those of the ancient glassworker (*Corning, NY, Corning Glass Center*).

p. 109 • Blown jug, opaque white, 6 inches (15.2 cm) (*Corning, NY, Corning Museum of Glass*).

- Blown glass bird, 1st century AD, 4.6 inches (11.7 cm) long with restored tail (*Corning, NY, Corning Museum of Glass*). The bird was a container for perfume or face powder (traces found), and the user had to break the end off the tail to reach the contents. It is an example of the subtlety of form obtainable by simple manipulation of the bubble on the end of a blowing iron. To complete it, the craftsman transfers it from the blowing iron to a metal rod (punty), attached underneath the bird, so that the beak and tail can be drawn out with tongs (see left-hand side of line drawing on p. 108).
- Mold-blown scent bottles were made in a variety of shapes, e.g. date, shell, birds, human heads. This example is from the British Museum.
p. 110 • For much of the length of the Nile, the land made fertile by annual inundations was a narrow strip, menaced by the desert behind (*R.L. Dalladay*).
- Peasants harvesting corn, painted relief, 3rd millenium BC, tomb at Saqqara.
- Unpainted relief, 3rd millenium BC, tomb of Mereruke, a high-ranking official. Two scribes checking estate accounts write on papyrus.
p. 111 • Some Roman emperors were portrayed as the hawk-headed Horus. The hawk's feathers suggest metal armor (*British Museum*).
- Charta Borgiana, AD 192–193 (*Naples, Archaeological Museum, Egyptian Gallery*).
- Painted relief from temple of Rameses II (1279–1213 BC), Abydos. The Nile deity carries on a tray the fruits of the earth, birds, and lotus flowers. Hanging from his arm are two ankhs, symbols of life (see illustration p. 113). Since the building of the Aswan High Dam, the Nile no longer floods every year.
p. 112 Decorative wall panel (see also pp. 98–99), Egyptian in style, mosaic of shaped pieces of glass and stone (**opus sectile**), Basilica of Junius Bassus, Rome, 4th century AD (*Rome, Museo Nazionale Romano*). It illustrates the enduring fascination Egypt held for the Romans.

Suggestions for further activities

1 Quintus says of Clemens (p. 95), "**vir fortis … est. fortūna semper eī favet.**" After reading the whole Stage, do you agree with Quintus? Do you consider good fortune or bravery more important?

2 Study the illustrations of different glassmaking techniques and find modern examples, e.g. bottles made in molds (you can see where the two halves of the mold join to each other and to the base); millefiori in paperweights; cut glass in tumblers, jugs, bowls, etc. Draw and label them.

3 If possible, arrange to visit a glassworks in operation, or a good gallery. Glassblowing has changed very little from the time it was first invented. There are frequently demonstrations in historical parks, like those at Williamsburg, VA; at Sturbridge, MA; the Black Creek Pioneer Village, in Toronto, ON; and especially the Corning, NY, Glass Center, where you can watch modern glassblowers at work and examine the museum's many examples of ancient glass. At the time of publishing, the Resident Advisor at the Corning Glass Center is William Gudenrath, who specializes in using ancient techniques to duplicate ancient glass.

4 Students might examine (from museum catalogues, from the text, etc.) and then copy specific vessels to fill a bulletin board "shelf" from Clemens' glass shop.

Vocabulary checklist (p. 112)

The genders of nouns are given for the first time in this checklist. Encourage students to learn the gender of nouns, especially those of the 3rd declension. The more familiar the students become with this, the more easily they will read the Latin of Unit 4. It is, however, not necessary to test gender on vocabulary tests. Make sure that students notice the new format for adjectives in future checklists.

nēmō is a compound of **nē** + **homō**, i.e. *no man*.

Phrases for discussion

annuit coeptis

incipe: dimidium facti est coepisse [Ausonius]

ubi mel, ibi apes

nemo in amore videt [*love is blind*]

nemo liber est qui corpori servit

pro deo et patria

quo vadis? [title of a novel and film set in Nero's Rome]

STAGE 19: Īsis

Cultural context
The worship of Isis: spring festival, initiation, spread of worship.

Story line
Aristo, a friend of Barbillus, takes Quintus to the spring festival in honor of Isis. Barbillus invites them on a crocodile hunt.

Main language features
- hic, ille
  e.g. *hic vir est Aristō. illa fēmina est Galatēa.*

- imperatives; **nōlī, nōlīte**.
  e.g. *iuvenēs! cēdite! nōlīte nōbīs obstāre!*
- vocative
  e.g. *ubi sunt latrōnēs, Eutyche?*

Sentence patterns
There are no new sentence patterns in this Stage.

Focus of exercises
1 **hic** and **ille**.
2 Recognition of cases.

Opening page (p. 113)

Illustration. Detail from the papyrus of Queen Nedjmet, *c.* 1050 BC (*British Museum*). This shows the Egyptian representation of Isis, holding a scepter in her right hand and an ankh (symbol of life) in her left. Above her head is the hieroglyph of a throne, her name in hieroglyphs. After studying the picture, read pp. 128–129 which give more information about Isis and provide a context for the model sentences.

Model sentences (pp. 114–115)

Story. The family of Aristo, a friend of Barbillus, watches the procession of Isis.

New vocabulary. castīgat, corōnās (new meaning), **rosārum**.

New language feature. hic: nominative and accusative singular in all genders, nominative and accusative plural in masculine and feminine.

The use of the genitive, first introduced in prepositional phrases in Stage 17, is extended here to include phrases where it is dependent upon a noun in the nominative or accusative. The students grasp this without the need for explanation.

Drawing 5 shows Isis in her likeness of the mother goddess Hathor, whose symbol is the disk of the sun encircled by horns. She is often shown as a cow.

Consolidation. Oral practice with phrases or sentences met here helps to establish the new characters and context, and forms a useful introduction to subsequent stories, especially **Aristō**, p. 116.

Further information. In depicting a preponderance of white garments in the pictures, we have followed the Herculaneum fresco of the Worship of Isis, and Ovid's promise to offer incense to Isis while clothed all in white (*Amores* 2.13).

Aristō (p. 116)

Story. Aristo's unhappiness is explained. His wife entertains noisy musicians and his daughter attracts disruptive satirical poets, both inimical to the quiet reflections of a tragic poet. The students will no doubt supply modern parallels.

First reading. Introduce each paragraph with oral practice of the relevant model sentence on p. 114, and read it aloud in Latin, asking comprehension questions to help the students understand the family and its conflicts over popular culture and serious art. Neither mother nor daughter shares Aristo's taste in literature; theirs is the popular culture of light music, novels, and verse which existed in the Hellenistic world side by side with more serious art.

Consolidation. Ask the students to identify and translate phrases incorporating the genitive. Invite them to write a diary entry in English for Galatea, Helena, or Aristo, based on this story and describing their lives and different points of view.

Illustrations

- The Roman theater at Alexandria, looking from behind the stage toward the auditorium which seated 800 spectators.
- Mosaic of playwright, late 2nd to early 3rd century AD (*Tunis, Bardo Museum*). The poet is perhaps the comic dramatist Menander, planning his play by reflecting on the masks of comic characters. Only one mask is visible here (top left).

diēs fēstus I (p. 117)

Story. Barbillus, unwilling to attend the spring festival, arranges for Quintus to go with Aristo and his family. As they approach the harbor, Galatea nags continually.

First reading. Help the students to recognize the joyful and expectant mood of the first paragraph by your Latin reading, and by drawing their attention to the language, e.g.: the lively effect of the two short sentences at the beginning; the heightened anticipation of the repeated **iam** (lines 1–2); the reference to the goddess as a person rather than a statue (line 2); and the excitement of the annual festival **sacerdōtēs … erat** (lines 2–4). Encourage students to visualize the scene.

Students could read the rest of the story on their own or in groups. Offer help only if necessary, e.g. with the word order of **viās … Alexandrīnī** (lines 10–11). If you keep a list of items the students find challenging, you can practice them orally at the beginning or end of subsequent lessons.

Consolidation. Ask the students to read the sentence **ego … numquam** (lines 6–7), emphasizing the contrast. Then ask them to translate other sentences with this shape which they have already met, e.g.:

> **sed illī erant multī, nōs paucī** (p. 79, line 21).
> **tabernāriī mihi pecūniam dant, ego eīs praesidium** (p. 96, Part II, lines 16–17).
> **tabernāriī Eutychum inimīcum putābant, Clēmentem vindicem** (p. 100, lines 18–19).

Students could then translate further sentences where the effect is not contrast, but emphasis, e.g.:

> **fenestrae erant frāctae, casa dīrepta** (p. 79, lines 24–25).
> **valvās ēvulsās vīdit, tabernam dīreptam** (p. 96, Part I, lines 5–6).
> **multī fūrēs ad hanc viam veniunt, multī latrōnēs** (p. 96, Part II, lines 14–15).

Illustration. Egyptian mummy portrait (*Stuttgart, Württembergisches Landesmuseum*), dated around AD 100, painted in encaustic on a panel, which was then cut down and glued into the mummy wrappings with bitumen, of which traces can be seen in the black splodges at bottom right and left. The inscription across the neck, *Eirene, daughter of S … May her soul rise before Osiris, the great god, forever*, is interesting for the Greek name combined with the Egyptian burial rite. She wears a green tunic, with a red mantle over her shoulder, a gold wreath of myrtle leaves and berries, and pearl earrings.

diēs fēstus II (pp. 118–119)

Story. Finding Aristo had forgotten to send a slave to keep good places for them at the temple of Augustus, Galatea dislodges two men.

First reading. If students need reassurance, then the questions could be done together or in groups. Otherwise, they should be able to provide reasonable answers by themselves in class, or as a homework assignment.

Consolidation. This is a good story for dramatization (starting from p. 117, line 13). Ask the students to make a collection of all the Latin verbs for speaking used in Parts I and II of the story, e.g. **inquit, vituperābat**.

Illustrations

This series of mummy paintings is remarkable for the youth of the subjects. It is possible that the paintings were prepared in life. However, census returns from Roman Egypt confirm the low life expectancy at the time. A number of mummies, like the young boy (last male figure), have been subjected to Computerized Axial Tomography (CAT) scans which reveal the correspondence of age between the body and the painting. From left to right:

- Man, encaustic on limewood, AD 80–100, from Hawara (*British Museum*), wearing white tunic with purple stripe, typical of men in mummy portraits, and white mantle.
- Young woman, encaustic on wood, AD 130–150, from Antinoopolis (*Paris, Louvre*), wearing dark blue tunic over white under-tunic with little purple triangles along the neckline and gold earrings in the shape of bunches of grapes.
- Curly-headed man, encaustic on wood, mid-3rd century AD, unknown provenance (*Paris, Louvre*), wearing white tunic with two small, dark decorations at the neck and dark red mantle.
- Girl, encaustic on wood, AD 117–138, from Antinoopolis (*Paris, Louvre*). The neck, shoulders, and pendant were initially painted and afterward covered in gold leaf. Her earrings have two pearls separated by a colored stone. Her hair is drawn back into a coiled bun and fixed in place with a gold pin.
- Woman, encaustic on limewood, AD 110–120, from Hawara (*British Museum*), wearing cyclamen-mauve tunic and mantle, gold hoop earrings set with three round emeralds, and two necklaces. The upper is of emeralds and gold, the lower of amethysts with a large central emerald from which hang two pearls.
- Man of Greek appearance, encaustic on wood, AD 130–161, provenance unknown (*Moscow, Pushkin Museum*), wearing white tunic and mantle.
- Young boy, encaustic on wood, AD 100–120, from Hawara (*British Museum*), wearing white tunic and mantle. The portrait is still framed in the mummy wrappings.

- Woman, tempera (water-based paint) and encaustic on limewood, AD 60–70, from er-Rubayat (*London, National Gallery*), wearing crimson tunic with a black stripe edged with gold, darker crimson mantle, gold ball earrings, and plaited gold chain round her neck above a gold and emerald necklace.

About the language 1: *hic* and *ille* (p. 120)

New language feature. The nominative and accusative cases of **hic** and **ille**.

Discussion. If students ask about a neuter plural form, confirm that it exists but has not yet occurred in the stories.

Consolidation. For further practice on **hic**, return to the model sentences (pp. 114–115) and ask the students to identify the case, number, and gender of each example of **hic** and its accompanying noun. **diēs fēstus II** (p. 118) can be used in the same way to practice **ille**. Students could be asked to practice **hic** and **ille** by exchanging **hic** for **ille** and vice versa. Alternatively, make up English sentences, e.g. "I was this girl," and ask what the Latin would be for "this" in the context of the sentence.

pompa (pp. 121–122)

Story. As the procession passes, Helena and Galatea make remarks about what they see, and the young men make remarks about them, eventually barging into Galatea. She criticizes Helena for siding with them, and Aristo for his lack of care.

First reading. This story may be taken as an amusing incident, or as a study of the family's characters, or as an illustration of the general point that people tend to notice what interests them. Read it straight through without comment, and then ask questions to encourage discussion.

Discussion

1 *Behavior and character.* What do you think of Galatea's behavior to her family and to the young men? What kinds of things does she say to each of them? Refer to the Latin. Is she fair to Aristo? Does Helena seem as quick to criticize her mother? (cf. **hic iuvenis tibi forte nocuit**, line 35). Which one of the family members says least in this scene? In what way is this significant? Is Aristo speaking to anyone in particular when he makes his remarks? Why is he an unhappy man?

2 *What people notice.* What features of the procession does Helena notice and comment on? What catches Galatea's eye? What reflection does she make after her comment on Isis' dress? Do the young men mind not having a good view of the procession? What do they comment on?

3 *The point of the story.* Which do you learn more about: the procession or the spectators? Do you find the story amusing? Give a reason.

Consolidation. Ask the students to sketch or diagram the procession, based on the model sentences (p. 115), this story, and the cultural context material (pp. 128–131). During discussion, students might compare this event with modern spring festivals, like Easter, May Day, Purim, or the Hindu festival of Holi.

Illustrations

- The image of Isis shows her in her likeness of the mother goddess Hathor, whose symbol is the disk of the sun encircled by horns. (Hathor is often shown as a cow.)
- Tragic mask in marble from Villa of Tiberius, Sperlonga, Italy.

This is a good point at which to complete the reading of the cultural material on pp. 130–131.

About the language 2: imperatives (p. 123)

New language features. Imperatives singular and plural, including **nōlī**, **nōlīte**.

Discussion. Make sure that students understand the reason for the infinitive in the negative commands.

Consolidation. After studying the note, ask the class which person in **pompa** (pp. 121–122) gave more orders than anyone else. Then ask students to collect all the instructions issued by the bossy Galatea in recent stories. You could give some orders yourself and invite volunteers to carry them out, e.g.: **exī! venī hūc! sedē! surge! dormīte! nōlīte dormīre! scrībite! nōlīte sedēre!** Then ask two or three students to give orders to the teacher and the class. A contest which eliminates those who react incorrectly to an order (a prize for the last one left) is an entertaining variation.

vēnātiō I (p. 124)

Story. Barbillus, leaving for a day's hunting with Quintus and Aristo, hesitates when his astrologer reminds him that it is an unlucky day. Against his better judgment he finally decides to go. Everything is ready at his farm by the Nile.

First reading. The language of this passage is straightforward. Maintain the pace, making sure the sequence of events is clear. Check understanding with a series of questions, e.g.:

> Where did Barbillus invite Quintus?
> What preparations did he make?
> What did Phormio take with him? Why?
> What caused Barbillus to hesitate?
> Why did he decide to go ahead? Give two reasons.
> Describe the scene at the farm.
> Make a list of the jobs Phormio had carried out.

The presence of the astrologer will need an explanation. It was common for the wealthy to keep astrologers in their households and consult them about domestic and business matters. It was easy for them to become a powerful influence if their predictions proved correct.

Discussion

1 *Hunting* can be an emotive topic. Encourage the students to see it from the viewpoint of the ancient world. It developed a young man's strength, bravery, and skill with weapons, and it was useful in a society where every public career required military service and command in the Roman army; for some it was one of the few ways of obtaining meat. The Ethiopians are present as the local experts in this kind of hunting. Why do you think Quintus was keen to proceed with this particular hunt?

2 *Astrology*. Ask students to think of a modern equivalent to the amulet. Discuss the continuing popularity of astrology. The serious scientific study of astronomy in the ancient world and the pseudoscience of astrology were developed by a priestly caste from Babylonia, the Chaldeans. Elicit from students the difference between the two. What or who persuades Barbillus to go on the hunt?

3 *Atmosphere*. This story leads to the death of Barbillus in Stage 20. Without revealing this, help the students to gain a sense of foreboding from: **perīculōsum est tibi** (lines 8–9); **Barbillus … rem diū cōgitāvit** (lines 10–11); the irony underlying **secūrī** (line 14); and the slaughter of the young goats. Why were they killed?

Consolidation. The range of persons and tenses makes this passage useful for reviewing verbs. Ask students to translate specific verbs from the passage, while keeping the passage in front of them, so that they can see the verb in context. Such verbs could be used as the basis for oral substitution practice. If short of time, select ten verbs and test them quickly at the end of the lesson.

The incidence of verbs accompanied by a dative has been increasing during the last few Stages. This passage contains three examples: **appropinquat** (line 9), **crēdēbat** (line 11), and **persuādēre** (line 13). This would be a good opportunity to study these examples in conjunction with the Language information section, p. 172.

Illustration. Detail of the Farnese Atlas, Hellenistic marble statue (*Naples, Archaeological Museum*).

vēnātiō II (p. 125)

Story. The hunters accidentally rouse a hippopotamus which overturns the boat carrying Barbillus and three slaves. The hunters drive away the crocodiles by throwing spears, but Barbillus is wounded in the shoulder.

First reading. Keep a lively pace in order to bring out the danger and excitement of the story, reading it with the class as far as **in aquam dēiēcit** (line 14). Then either continue with the class in the same way, or have volunteers act out the remainder (having ascertained the meaning in their groups), or have the most talented artist of the group draw the narrative on the board.

Discussion

1 *Style*. Lines 7–10 are the climax of the first part of this story. Who are the main participants? Devise a really stylish English translation for the sentence **magna erat fortitūdō … Aethiopum** (lines 8–9). Who does the writer suggest will win? Is that what actually happens?

2 *Barbillus' accident*. What was the cause? Does he seem to be on good terms with his slaves? For instance, check the text where he and Phormio interact in **vēnātiō I** and **II**. Taking into account the type of wound Barbillus suffered, his time in the water, his state of mind, and the astrologer's warning, what do you think will happen to him?

Consolidation

1 Pick out the relative clauses and ask students to identify the noun being described, giving its gender and number, and then translate the sentence.

2 Ask the students to look back over **vēnātiō I** and **II** and select and translate three sentences which represent significant moments in the story. What do they think will happen to Barbillus next?

Illustrations

- Scenes of the Nile peopled by pygmies were popular in the Roman world (*Rome, Museo Nazionale*). In this mosaic do you find the animals lifelike? Do the hunters look as if they will overwhelm the animals? Is the overall impact of the mosaic comic, realistic, or fanciful?
- Amulet to ward off evil (*Naples, Archaeological Museum*), depicting hippopotamus god, molded in "faience," a popular material made of a turquoise glaze on a molded sandy or earthenware core.

About the language 3: vocative case (p. 126)

New language feature. The vocative case.

Discussion. Vocatives have appeared regularly enough that this note should cause no problems. Students are pleased to note that the vocative is usually no different from the nominative, but still intrigued at the instances where a person's name could change its form if s/he was being addressed. (Those who have seen Shakespeare's *Julius Caesar* will cite **et tu, Brute?** as the world's most famous vocative.) They will also be pleased to know that the vocative completes the list of cases in the declension of a noun.

Consolidation. Both **diēs fēstus** (pp. 117–118) and **pompa** (pp. 121–122) contain many examples of the vocative and imperative. Students could be asked to find these.

Illustration. Detail of wall painting from the temple of Isis at Pompeii, showing crocodile lurking in vegetation, lotus plants nearby, native reed-thatched hut in background, shrines in foreground.

Practicing the language (p. 127)

Exercise 1. Complete the sentences by selecting the correct form of **hic** and **ille**, using the Vocabulary at the end of the book to check the gender of nouns if necessary.

Exercise 2. Recognize the case of an unfinished noun in the context of the sentences, and add the appropriate case ending, using the table of nouns in the Language information (pp. 154–155).

Language information: review

Review nouns (pp. 154–157). Study the notes on pp. 154–156 and work through exercises 12–14 on p. 157.

Review adjectives (pp. 158–159).

Work on Verbs with the dative (p. 172) has already been indicated.

Cultural context material (pp. 128–131)

Content. The importance of Isis in Egyptian religion, her worship, her wider appeal in the Roman world.

Suggestions for discussion

1   *The worship of Isis.* Help the students to build up a picture of how Isis was worshipped at the spring festival from the stories and the cultural context section, and gather details of daily worship from the illustration on p. 130 and from **Clēmēns tabernārius** (pp. 100–101). Some students may be able to compare the festival with modern religious celebrations in this country and in other parts of the world.

2   *Comparison of the worship of Isis with Christianity.* The cult of Isis spread through the Roman world at the same time as the spread of Christianity. There are similarities because the early Christian church tended to assimilate other religions' ideas and practices in keeping with its own outlook. Students who are conversant with Christianity may be able to identify similarities, e.g.:

> repentance, fasting, and baptism;
>
> hope of life after death;
>
> The Trinity and the linking of Isis, Osiris, and Horus;
>
> sacramental meals and private meditation as a way of communing with the godhead;
>
> the use of incense, flowers, light, music, choirs, and the veneration of relics.

Unlike Christianity, the cult of Isis did not survive. Possible reasons for this include:

> it was expensive to become a follower of Isis;
>
> there was no historical foundation for the myths about Isis, Osiris, and Horus, and no well-defined set of beliefs;
>
> Isis worship did not require an ethical or moral commitment in daily life;
>
> it lost its distinctive identity because it accommodated other gods, whereas the demands of Christianity were uncompromising.

3   *Different religions today.* In some circumstances it may be possible for students to share their own diverse experiences. Which religious festivals are associated with public holidays in Canada and the United States today? Which of them are filled with fun?

Further information

In the Greco-Roman world of the first century AD, mystery religions exercised a pervasive influence. The cult of Isis, described in Stages 18 and 19, was one of these religions and it is particularly interesting for two reasons. First, it was the religion that Alexandria passed on to the ancient world. When the Ptolemaic rulers imposed on the city a new official state cult, that of Serapis, they incorporated into it the old Egyptian myth of Osiris–Isis. The official cult image of Serapis, fashioned by the Greek sculptor Bryaxis and housed in the Serapeum designed by Parmeniscus, gave this ancient Egyptian god a Greek form. Nevertheless, it was the more primitive, life-giving Isis who exerted a stronger hold on people's affections. It was Isis rather than Serapis whose worship spread from Alexandria throughout the Mediterranean. It was the cult of Isis, the mother goddess who gave life to the land and all its creatures and who offered hope of life after death, that received official Roman recognition from the Emperor Caligula and was held in high regard by the Flavian emperors.

Secondly, it is interesting to observe resemblances between the worship of Isis and Christianity. See Suggestions for discussion, above.

The **nāvigium Īsidis** was celebrated every year, after the winter storms, at the beginning of the sailing season; it was performed not only at Alexandria, but wherever a temple of Isis was situated near the sea.

For a vivid description of Isis and her worship from ancient times, see Apuleius *Metamorphoses* XI.3–4, 9–11, and 16–17. For a description of the annual festivals celebrating the resurrection of Osiris, see Juvenal *Satires* VI.532–541 and VIII.29–30.

Illustrations

p. 128
- Sistra from Pompeii (*Naples, Archaeological Museum*). Sistra were shaken to repel the forces of evil or to express joy or mourning. The bronze rods jingle when shaken from side to side. Sometimes rattles are used in the modern orchestra.
- Woman playing a sistrum; detail from mosaic of the seasons, Carthage, 4th century AD (*British Museum*), representing the month of November when the festival took place to celebrate the finding of Osiris' body.
- Statuette of Isis, 4th century BC (*British Museum*), providing the universal image of mother and child. Isis wears on her head her throne hieroglyph and (just visible underneath it) the **ūraeus**, a rearing cobra which symbolized kingship.

p. 129
- Isis and her brother Osiris, relief with original painting, 13th century BC, from the temple of Seti I at Abydos, headquarters of the worship of Osiris. He wears the white crown of Upper Egypt adorned with feathers. Isis wears the horns and sun disk of Hathor above a vulture headdress. The triad of Isis, Horus, and Osiris represented the powers of creation and rebirth.
- Bronze coin, 2nd century AD, from Alexandria (*British Museum*). Isis Pharia grasps the top corners of a square sail as it billows out before her. The Pharos shows the ramp leading up to the entrance, the statues of Tritons on the corners of the bottom story, and the statue on the apex of the building. The coin reflects the importance of shipping to the economic life of Alexandria, and of Isis as the divine protector of the shipping trade.
- Detail of mosaic, showing the Nile flooding around a small island, about 80 BC. Two men chat in the doorway of a reed hut while their companion watches the cow, and another rows a reed boat. Lotuses can be seen among the vegetation in the water and ibises perch on the roof (*photograph by Michael Holford, Palestrina, Museo Prenestino Barberiniano*).

p. 130 Wall painting from Herculaneum, showing morning ceremony of Isis (*Naples, Archaeological Museum*). The temple at the top of the steps is flanked by palm trees and sphinxes crowned with lotus. The shaven-headed high priest in the doorway holds Nile water in a sacred vessel, ready to pour the morning libations on all the altars in the precinct; the priest and priestess beside him are shaking sistra; below them a priest with a wand conducts a choir of men and women; another priest fans the flames on a small horned altar garlanded with flowers, ready for the offerings of milk, honey, or herbs; a priest and priestess (front left) shake sistra; the standing priest (front right) carries a rod, the seated one plays a flute. A sacred ibis, symbol of healing, has settled on the back of the left-hand sphinx, two others wander in the foreground.

p. 131 • For the Egyptian Isis, see notes on opening page (p. 64 of this manual).

• Isis welcoming Io to Egypt. Detail of wall painting from temple of Isis in Pompeii (*Naples, Archaeological Museum*). The worship of Isis was established in Rome by the 1st century BC. Though periodically banned from the city itself, the cult was favored by the Flavian emperors. It was virtually dead by the 4th century AD.

• Isis was the goddess of fruitfulness. In her temple in Pompeii were found fish and eggs as well as the walnuts, grain, and bread shown here (*Photo Alinari*).

p. 132 • Model hippopotamus, made of "Egyptian faience" (see note on amulet on p. 70 of this manual) (*British Museum*).

Suggestions for further activities

1 Read to the class extracts from the novel by Apuleius, *The Golden Ass* (Penguin), which deals with Isis in chapters 17–18.

2 Imagine that you are Clemens and write a dialogue in which you explain to Quintus why you are attracted to the worship of Isis.

3 Quintus says of Clemens (p. 95) **vir fortis … est. fortūna semper eī favet.** Basing your answer on the events in Units 1 and 2, write a journal entry in which you consider whether you agree with Quintus. Do you consider good fortune or bravery more important? Would Clemens consider Fortuna or Isis more responsible for his good luck?

4 Study the Nile scenes (pp. 125, 126, 129, and 151), comparing them with the photograph of the Nile (p. 110), and answer the following questions:

What facts about the Nile can you deduce from the pictures?

What fantastic elements do you detect?

What do you think made these scenes so popular among the Romans of Italy?

Which scene do you prefer and why?

Vocabulary checklist (p. 132)

fortasse, **forte**, and **fortis** often are confused by students.

Phrases for discussion

in loco parentis

vita non est vivere sed valere vita est [Martial]

vox clamantis in deserto [motto of Dartmouth College, NH]

qui bene amat, bene castigat

quot homines, tot sententiae

medice, cura te ipsum

cogito, ergo sum [Descartes]

vox populi, vox dei

audi, vide, tace, si vis vivere in pace

STAGE 20: medicus

Cultural context
Alexandria: medicine, mathematics, astronomy, inventions.

Story line
Conflicting treatments, provided for Barbillus' shoulder by the Greek doctor and the astrologer, result in Barbillus' death. Quintus is asked to look for his son in Britain.

Main language features
- present participle
  e.g. *ancillae prope lectum stābant, lacrimantēs.*

- **is** and **ea** in the genitive, dative, and accusative
  e.g. *Petrō, postquam dē vulnere Barbillī audīvit, statim ad vīllam eius festīnāvit.*

Sentence patterns
increased complexity of sentence structure: "stringing" of two parallel subordinate clauses
e.g. *servī, quī Barbillum portābant, ubi cubiculum intrāvērunt, in lectum eum lēniter posuērunt.*

Focus of exercises
1 Present participle.
2 Imperative.
3 Relative clauses.

Opening page (p. 133)

Illustration. Sealstone made of sard, a kind of cornelian, Roman, 1st–2nd century AD, showing doctor (right) examining the swollen stomach of a standing youth. Asclepius, god of medicine (left), leans on his staff, around which his familiar serpent is coiled (*British Museum*).

Model sentences (p. 134)

Story. Barbillus is carried to his bed. The astrologer bursts in while Phormio runs for a doctor.

New language feature. Present participles in the nominative case.

New vocabulary. lectum (new meaning), **medicum**.

First reading. Students quickly work out how to translate the sentences correctly. They have already met several examples in previous Stages (e.g. **cachinnāns, susurrāns**). As usual, postpone formal discussion until the language note, p. 137.

Consolidation. Recapitulation of selected sentences at the beginning or end of the next few lessons will be necessary to establish the new form. Pave the way for the important notion of agreement by asking, for example, of sentence 1, "*Who* were carrying Barbillus?"

remedium astrologī (p. 135)

Story. Phormio tries in vain to staunch the blood with an improvised bandage, then cobwebs. When the astrologer bursts in with recriminations, Barbillus asks Quintus to send for Petro the doctor.

First reading. At the start, **ego** reminds the reader that Quintus is telling the story. The first paragraph presents a challenge with the rapidly switching tenses. Students might be asked to comment on the word order of the last sentence, i.e. the effectiveness of putting **sanguis** last.

The next two sections of the story, **servī … collocāvit** (lines 6–15) and **astrologus ancillās … remedium est** (lines 16–24), could be approached by students on their own or in groups, or by the teacher stopping at intervals and calling for translation or asking comprehension questions (e.g. "What three things does Phormio do in the first half of the story?" "What is the astrologer's response to the news of the accident?" "What does he say about his remedy?" "What request does Barbillus make?" "Whose ear would be **aurem meam**?").

The penultimate sentence, **Phormiōnem … ēmīsī**, often causes difficulty. Give help by reading it through to the end, eliciting the significance of word endings as you go. Reinforce this sentence pattern with other examples the students have already met, e.g. **servum, quī tam fortis … fuerat, līberāvī** (Stage 16, p. 67, lines 8–9).

Help the class to appreciate the suspense of the final section, and the contrasting purposes of the steward and the astrologer, which the writer emphasizes by the word order of the last sentence.

Discussion
1 *Focus of story.* Why do you think the writer has given the story this title? How does it relate to the last two words of the passage? Is the writer being ironic?
2 *Phormio.* What kind of person is Phormio? (Celsus, a medical writer in the first century AD, gives a list of coagulants which includes cobwebs. See also Pliny *NH* 30.112. In fact, the protein they contain also deters gangrene.)
3 *The astrologer.* Ask students to quote the words of the astrologer which show he thinks he was right in his earlier warnings. Do you agree with him?
4 *Quintus.* In what tone of voice did Quintus ask **habēsne remedium** (line 19)? What was his previous attitude to the astrologer? Has it changed? Refer to **vēnātiō I**, p. 124, line 10.
5 *Barbillus.* What do you think Barbillus' attitude to the astrologer is now?

Consolidation. If the class had difficulty with the last paragraph, students could be asked to write a translation of these lines. The first three paragraphs contain examples of the present, imperfect, perfect, and pluperfect tenses. Students could be asked to find examples of each.

Illustration. Detail from mosaic representing unswept floor of dining room (*Rome, Vatican Museums*). Another detail is illustrated in Unit 1 (p. 87).

Petrō (p. 136)

Story. After trouncing the astrologer, the Greek doctor cleans and stitches Barbillus' wound, and advises quiet and rest. Quintus stays to help Barbillus with his business affairs, and learns his sad story.

First reading. Guide the students through the story by the use of lively Latin reading and comprehension questions (e.g. "What does Petro see and what does Petro do in the first paragraph?" "List the medical treatment he gives Barbillus." "What does he warn Quintus?" "How does Quintus spend much of his time after this?").

Discussion. Was Petro right to be angry with the astrologer? In what ways was Petro's treatment similar to modern medicine? Quote the appropriate Latin (**cutem … perītē cōnseruit**).

This story emphasizes the scientific competence of Petro: he knows the importance of hygiene and demonstrates surgical skill. Vinegar is intended to suppress a flow of blood and also served as an antiseptic (Majno, pp. 186 and 362). He appreciates that healing is a natural process. Ask students to quote the Latin that shows this. Then ask them to contrast this with the astrologer's assertion in the previous story (p. 135, line 20). Science opposes magic in this story, but encourage the students to consider why the astrologer chooses a mouse for his treatment. He was correct in attributing the remedy to tradition. Pliny, in his *Natural History*, frequently praised the medicinal properties of mice (especially in Book 29.15 and in Book 30.26, 29, 30).

This faith in the vitalizing qualities of mice was particularly strong in Egypt. When the Nile receded after its flood peak, mice were suddenly seen everywhere—as the elder Pliny noted—jumping around in the mud, and they were thought to have been spontaneously created by the legendary, life-giving water of the Nile (*NH* 9.179).

The desiccated body of an early Egyptian boy, buried in the desert, preserved in his intestine the remains of his last medicine: "a skinned mouse, young, well chewed, and mixed with vegetables" (Majno, p. 138).

You might also compare the scene of Quintus in the last paragraph with him listening to Cogidubnus and then telling him about his own experiences, as he is doing now: Cogidubnus and Barbillus as father figures in his life, perhaps, after the death of his own father.

Consolidation. Ask the students to reread one passage from the story, e.g. **mē ita … afflīxerat** (line 20–end), raising any queries or uncertainties they have. Then ask for an oral translation of selected sentences. Students could also list the things Petro does in lines 7–19 and write down which ones are good medical practice.

Illustration. Petro stitching the wound.

About the language 1: present participles (p. 137)

New language feature. Present participle in nominative and accusative cases.

Discussion. Work through the first three paragraphs with the class. If the students work at paragraph 4 on their own, you can circulate identifying any problems requiring further help.

Consolidation. Ask the students to identify the present participles in the model sentences and say which noun each describes.

**fortūna crūdēlis (pp. 138–139)

Story. Barbillus' son persuades his mother to accompany him on a voyage to Greece, against the advice of the astrologer. The ship is wrecked and she is drowned. Barbillus refuses to have his son back.

First reading. Divide the class into groups of two or three students and have them attempt the comprehension questions on p. 139. Encourage the students to look at the questions one at a time and then search for each answer in the text, rather than reading the entire story and then attempting to answer the questions.

Discussion

1   *Family conflict.* This topic needs sensitive handling. After students have read the story (alone or in groups) and answered the questions, they might like to discuss the family conflict in this story. With whom do they sympathize? What is their opinion of Plotina? Would they have acted differently? Did Rufus get what he deserved? Was Barbillus' reaction justified? Have they had similar disagreements?

2   *Sailing in the Mediterranean.* Remind students of the significance of the spring festival of Isis which they read about in the previous Stage. Seaways reopened in the spring after almost total closure in the winter months. Students living in the Great Lakes area will be aware of similar excitement when the St Lawrence Seaway opens. Shipwrecks played a significant part in ancient literature, e.g. the *Odyssey*, the *Aeneid*, and St Paul's journey to his trial in Rome (*Acts* 27). If any students have experienced sudden storms while traveling by boat, they could also comment.

If students need review in verbs that take the dative, the last three paragraphs of this story contain sentences with **crēdō**, **persuādeō**, **appropinquō**, and **pāreō**. As the latter is new, students might be asked to deduce this information about **pāreō** from its context in the penultimate sentence.

Illustration. Mosaic of merchant ship, late 2nd century BC (*Tunisia, Sousse Museum*). The ship is driven by oars as well as the wind. A decorative dolphin projects at the prow. Ribbons are hung on the mast and above the helmsman's reed cabin at the stern to indicate the direction of the wind. The vessel has eyes, either to see the way or to ward off the evil eye, a feature seen on many Mediterranean boats today.

About the language 2: *eum, eam,* etc. (p. 140)

New language feature. The genitive, dative, and accusative cases of **is** and **ea**, in the singular and the plural.

Discussion. After studying the explanation and the examples, pick out instances from the stories, and ask the students to translate them in their context, e.g.:

> **servī … eum lēniter posuērunt** (p. 135, lines 6–7)
> **Petrō … ad vīllam eius festīnāvit** (p. 136, lines 1–2)
> **eam in vulnus collocāvit** (p. 136, line 8)
> **necesse est eī** (p. 136, line 21)
> **negōtium eius administrāns** (p. 136, line 25)
> **fortūna eum … afflīxerat** (p. 136, line 29)
> **nāvis, quae eōs vehēbat** (p. 139, line 26)
> **tempestās eam obruit** (p. 139, line 27)

If you elicit from the students that some of the corresponding English pronouns—*he, him, his, they, them, their*, etc.—are among the few English words to possess cases, they are more likely to see the inflections as a "natural" feature of language.

   Rather than teaching the students the chart, you may wish to encourage them to learn the meaning of each form directly, as they would an item of vocabulary. For example, students may learn that **eum** means "him/it," that **eam** means "her/it," and that **eōs** means "them," etc. As the students have already seen many examples of these forms, they may find this a more effective strategy for fluent reading.

Consolidation. When making up further examples, give the students a preliminary sentence to establish the context. If you give students English sentences containing pronouns and ask them to translate the pronoun, allow them to use the chart on p. 140 initially and then see if they can manage without it.

astrologus victor I (pp. 140–141)

Story. The astrologer visits Barbillus on his sickbed and tries to undermine his confidence in the doctor with slanderous statements about his poor record and his greed for money. Barbillus refuses to listen.

First reading. After hearing the passage read in Latin, the students should be able to translate it in pairs or groups. Afterward, you could check understanding by putting some questions on the board for them to answer in writing, e.g.:
1 Which sentence shows how the astrologer and Petro felt about each other?
  2 Give the Latin word which is the opposite of **inimīcī** (line 2).
  3 Translate the sentence **ad cubiculum … veniēbat** (lines 6–7).
  4 Make a list of the lies the astrologer tells about Petro.
  5 What had Petro done to excite such hatred? If necessary, refer the students to the first scene with Petro and the astrologer (p. 136).
  6 What instructions of the astrologer made Barbillus **anxius** (line 13)?
  7 Why did the astrologer hatch a plot?
  8 What do you think he plans to do?

Consolidation

1 Ask the students to read aloud in Latin the astrologer's speech to Barbillus with appropriate expression. A written translation of line 9–end in appropriate English could be set for homework.
2 The third paragraph contains some superlatives and a comparative if students need review on these forms.

astrologus victor II (p. 141)

Story. The astrologer says that, in a dream, the young slave who was killed in the riot has given him a special remedy, and so Barbillus allows the astrologer to treat him. The wound deteriorates, the astrologer flees, and Barbillus gives Quintus his final message for his son.

First reading. Take the students through the first part of the passage, as far as **ad cubiculum arcessīvit** (line 13), giving help as necessary. The astrologer's speech presents a challenge because of the absence of nominatives from many sentences. The rest of the story could be read in groups or pairs.

Discussion

1 *Beliefs about astrology.* What is it that makes Barbillus believe in the astrologer? Encourage the students to recall his predictions in **vēnātiō I** (p. 124, lines 8–9) and **fortūna crūdēlis** (p. 138, lines 16–17). Why do you think Barbillus refuses to recall Petro?

2 *Letter to Rufus.* What do you think this contained?

3 *Responsibility.* Who (or what) was ultimately to blame for Barbillus' death? (Note Part I, lines 13–14, **quamquam dolor cotīdiē ingravēscēbat.**)

Ask the students to read aloud in Latin the astrologer's speech to Barbillus with appropriate expression. Why do you think this was a particularly effective dream to tell Barbillus?

If there is time, you might ask the students to think about how the astrologer has been represented in Parts I and II of this story, and why the writer has done this. The first line of Part I labels him **vir ingeniī prāvī**. Has he been shown to be so up to this point? Refer to lines where he has tried to help Barbillus. What verbs are used to describe him entering rooms (e.g. **cucurrit** in **vēnātiō I**, line 4; and **irrūpit** in **remedium astrologī**, line 17, and **astrologus victor II**, line 1)? What kind of person is shown here? Emotional? Excitable? In **astrologus victor**, the astrologer is a man of evil character. (He lies about Petro and probably lies about his dream. Do students believe he had such a dream?) Does the character label at the beginning of the story suggest he has always been this way? Why has he never been given a name?

The pathos in the death of Barbillus, though reminiscent of the death of Caecilius at the end of Unit 1, is intended to be more mature and to touch on deeper emotional levels. There are no heroics, only the sadness of wisdom that comes too late. Barbillus' final gesture is one of reparation for his failure to forgive and to put away bitterness.

Consolidation. Ask the students to identify all the dative cases in the passage and translate the sentences containing them. There are examples of the vocative (**domine**, **mī Quīnte**) and the second to last paragraph contains imperatives, positive and negative.

Illustration. Papyrus letter, 1st century AD, from Alexandria (*British Museum*) reading: Prokleios to his good friend Pekysis greetings. You will do well if, at your own risk, you sell to my friend Sotas such high-quality goods as he will tell you he needs, for him to bring to me at Alexandria. Know that you will have to deal with me about the cost. Greet all your family from me. Farewell.

Practicing the language (pp. 142–143)

Exercise 1. Complete the sentences with the correct form of present participle, selecting between nominative and accusative, singular and plural. This exercise is demanding. Help students by asking, "What noun does the participle describe? What is the case/number of that noun? Which then is the matching participle?"

Exercise 2. Complete the sentences with the correct form of the imperative.

Exercise 3. Translation passage practicing the relative clause. It will help students to recognize clause boundaries if you first read them the passage in Latin. Remind students that the punctuation and the position of the relative pronoun and the verb usually help them to recognize where clauses begin and end.

Illustration. Head of young man, in wax, egg, and oil on limewood, AD 80–120, from Hawara (*British Museum*). He is shown naked, which suggests a life devoted to exercise in the Greek gymnasium.

Cultural context material (pp. 144–149)

Content. The section about medicine is best studied in conjunction with **Petrō** (p. 136). The further information about mathematics, astronomy, and engineering could be compared with the pseudoscience of astrology as demonstrated in the stories.

Suggestions for discussion

1 *Science and superstition.* How can advanced scientific knowledge coexist with a belief in astrology? Do you find these stories convincing? Are there modern parallels?
2 *The Hippocratic oath.* What problems confront modern doctors in following these principles? Relevant ethical issues include confidentiality, euthanasia, abortion, and the use of injections for the death penalty in some of the states in the USA.

Further information

Scholars working, during both the Greek and Roman periods, at the Great Library in the Museum lived in apartments or dormitories connected with the Museum. This was built by Ptolemy I as one of the earliest known "research institutes." The Museum contained, besides the Great Library, study and meeting rooms, botanical and zoological gardens, dining halls, and colonnades that allowed scholars, in a typically Greek way, to stroll, talk, and debate in the open air.

All the scholars at the Museum were men and women of letters. Some of them pioneered in the new area of knowledge we now call science, presenting new theorems and hypotheses in mathematics, astronomy, or medicine. Particularly interesting are the calculations and inventions of Aristarchus, Eratosthenes, Archimedes, Ctesibius, Euclid, and Hero. Not only scientists and mathematicians but also poets, such as Callimachus, Apollonius Rhodius, and Theocritus, were encouraged. Hypatia of Alexandria was the most famous female mathematician, astronomer, and philosopher of antiquity.

No one knows what happened to the books in either the Serapeum Library (in the Egyptian quarter in the southwestern part of the city) or the larger Great Library (in the Greek quarter in the northern part of the city). Various stories of the burning of the Libraries at different times have been challenged (see Canfora). Yet the institution of a state library, first known from Alexandria, now flourishes in magnificent collections like that of the Library of Congress, Washington, DC. The Egyptian government and UNESCO are responsible for a major new library in Alexandria, billed as a revival of the ancient Library of Alexandria.

Illustrations

p. 144 • For sealstone, see note on p. 133.
p. 145 • Terracotta model of internal organs, 3rd–1st century BC (*British Museum*), dedicated either in hope of, or in gratitude for, a cure.
 • Relief of medical instruments, time of Trajan, temple at Komombo on the Nile.
 • Bleeding cup, bronze (*British Museum*). Celsus, 1st century AD, explains that burning lint was placed inside the vessel which was then applied over an incision in the skin. The vacuum drew the blood into the cup.

p. 146 • Relief from Tomb 100, Isola Sacra.
   • Roman bone saw in bronze, 1st–3rd century AD (*British Museum*).
   • Oculist's stamp, 1st–3rd century AD (*British Museum*). The remedies include "saffron ointment for soreness" and "saffron ointment for scratches and running eyes, prepared by Junius Taurus from a prescription of Pacius."
   • Set of Roman surgical instruments, 1st century AD (*British Museum*), found together in Italy. Top row from left: catheters, rectal speculum. Middle row from left: instrument cases, three spatulae for mixing and applying ointment, six scoops and spoons, eight probes, forceps, and hooks, one double-ended traction hook, two bone chisels. Bottom row from left: palette for grinding medicines, two plus four spatulae with a folding knife below, five handles for scalpels of which the blades have rusted away; the oval ends (at right) are blunt dissectors for pushing apart the incision.

p. 147 • Diagram of Eratosthenes' experiment.

p. 148 • Part of astronomical treatise called *The Art of Eudoxus*, first half of 2nd century BC, found in the temple of Serapis (*Paris, Louvre, photograph Réunion des Musées Nationaux*).
   • Diagram of Hero's steam turbine.

p. 149 • Statue of Hypatia of Alexandria, 4th–5th century AD.

p. 150 • The pyramids of Gizeh outside Cairo. From left to right: the tombs of Menkaure, Khafre, and Khufu (140m high), 3rd millenium BC.

Suggestions for further activities

1 The teacher could write the following epigram from Martial (I.47) on the board and help the students to read and appreciate it. Some may like to attempt a verse translation, perhaps in limerick form. They might then discuss whether such jokes were justified, or try writing another of their own, or compare English jokes about doctors.

   nuper erat medicus, nunc est vespillo Diaulus; vespillo *undertaker*
   quod vespillo facit, fecerat et medicus.
   On Diaulus: Previously a doctor, presently an undertaker,
   What he does in his new job, he used to do in his old.

2 In groups, choose one of the scientific developments (e.g. pulley, lever, concave mirror, cog wheels, etc.) based upon research in the ancient world. Explain to the class, with illustrations, the modern development you have chosen, why it is important, and the original discovery that made it possible. Invite your science and technology teachers to attend your presentation and comment.

3 Draw or make a model of one of the Alexandrian inventions and demonstrate it to the class. Invite your science and technology teachers to attend your presentation.

Vocabulary checklist (p. 150)

You may wish to point out that 3rd declension nouns ending in -**us**, such as **vulnus**, are neuter.

Phrases for discussion

ars gratia artis
ars longa, vita brevis
veritas vos liberabit
post mortem
stans pede in uno [Horace]

Other illustrations

Language information (p. 151). Detail, mosaic of a Nile scene, from House of the Faun, Pompeii (*Naples, Archaeological Museum*).

Front cover. "Gayer-Anderson" cat (see note on p. 59 of this manual).

Language information

About the language (pp. 154–177)

This section provides a reference and review for students. It collects and organizes various grammatical features such as the cases of nouns, pronouns, and adjectives, and the persons and tenses of verbs. It also amplifies certain grammatical points, such as sentence structure, from the students' readings.

The exercises in these notes may be used for oral or written work at whatever point in Unit 2 you believe students can most usefully, confidently, and successfully complete them. Before using or assigning any exercise, check to make sure that it does not include features yet to be explained in formal language notes, e.g. neuter plurals in a noun exercise or pluperfect tense in a verb exercise. In addition, the notes and exercises are suitable for a review at the end or the beginning of a year of Latin study. They are more effective in developing comprehension skills than memorization of isolated paradigm charts.

Vocabulary (pp. 178–195)

This section is a cumulated vocabulary for the entire Unit. It does not include words from Unit 1 which do not appear in Unit 2. The format and content are explained in notes on pp. 178–179 of the students' textbook. Note that concepts such as gender and genitive for nouns, adjectives, and pronouns are outlined in various Stages of this Unit, and it may be wise to wait until these have been met before attempting any formal discussion of this introductory explanation.

Linguistic synopsis of Unit 2

This synopsis follows the same plan and is designed for the same purposes as the Unit 1 linguistic synopsis described on p. 99 of the Unit 1 Teacher's Manual. When reading a Stage with a class, teachers are strongly advised to concentrate on the features dealt with in that Stage's language note(s), rather than attempting discussion and analysis of the other linguistic features listed here. LI = Language information.

Stage	*Place of* Linguistic feature	*language note etc.*
13	infinitive + **volō**, **nōlō**, **possum**	13
	present tense of **volō**, **nōlō**, **possum**	13, LI
	-que	13
	perfect passive participle	21
	clauses with **quamquam** and **simulac**	LI
	nominative singular of 2nd declension neuter nouns	18, LI
	omission of verb in second of two clauses	LI
	clauses with **ubi** (= *when*)	LI
	sēcum	LI
	apposition (nominative)	
	nominative predicative adjective	
14	attributive adjective (met from Stage 3): agreement of case and number	14, LI
	infinitive + **decōrum**, **difficile**, etc.	
	prepositional phrases	14, LI
	ablative singular and plural (in prepositional phrases)	14, LI
	vocative in -**ī**	19, LI
	nōlī (one example)	19
	imperative plural (one example)	19
	present participle	20
	ipse	
	apposition (accusative)	
	accusative predicative adjective	
15	relative clauses with nominative singular and plural and accusative singular of **quī**	15, LI
	imperfect of **possum**, **volō**, **nōlō**	15, LI
	infinitive + **dēbeō**	
	appropinquō + dative	LI
	omission of verb in first of two clauses (one example)	LI
16	pluperfect (in relative clause)	16
	infinitive + **audeō**	
	relative clauses with accusative plural of **quī**	
	relative clauses in sentences with subject omitted	

17	genitive singular and plural (in prepositional phrases)	17, LI
	obstō + dative	LI
	DATIVE + VERB word order	LI
	increased incidence of VERB + NOMINATIVE word order (from Stage 3)	LI
	increased complexity in subordinate clauses	LI
	pluperfect in main clause	
	infinitive + **soleō**, **coepī**, **melius est**	

18	adjective (met from Stage 3): agreement of gender	18, LI
	nominative and accusative singular and plural of neuter nouns	18, LI
	increased incidence of 4th and 5th declension nouns	LI
	increased incidence of verbs with dative	LI
	genitive + nominative (one example)	LI
	genitive + accusative (one example)	LI
	omission of verb in first of two clauses (met in Stage 15)	LI
	DATIVE + ACCUSATIVE + VERB word order	LI
	ACCUSATIVE + NOMINATIVE + VERB word order	LI
	"nesting" of one subordinate clause inside another (**e.g. ubi ā templō**, **in quō cēnāverat**, **domum redībat**, **amīcum cōnspexit accurrentem**)	
	ACCUSATIVE + DATIVE + VERB word order	
	clauses with **ut** (= *as*)	

19	genitive + nominative and accusative (from Stage 18)	LI
	genitive of adjective	LI
	hic (met from Stage 8)	19, LI
	ille (met from Stage 9)	19, LI
	imperative singular (from Stage 10) and plural (from Stage 14)	19, LI
	nōlī (from Stage 14) and **nōlīte**	19
	vocative (from Stages 11 and 14)	19, LI
	fīō + predicative nominative	

20	present participle (met from Stage 14)	20
	oblique cases of **is** (from Stage 7)	20, LI
	descriptive genitive (one example)	22
	"stringing" arrangement of two parallel subordinate clauses (**e.g. servī**, **quī Barbillum portābant**, **ubi cubiculum intrāvērunt**, **in lectum eum lēniter posuērunt**)	
	increased incidence of predicative adjective	

The following terms are used in Unit 2. Numerals indicate the Stage in which each term is first used. LI = Language information section.

Term	Stage
infinitive	13
adjective	14
agree(ment)	14
number	14
ablative	14
relative clause	15
relative pronoun	15
pluperfect	16
genitive	17
gender	18
masculine	18
feminine	18
neuter	18
imperative	19
vocative	19
present participle	20
positive (adjective)	LI
pronoun	LI
antecedent	LI
1st, 2nd, 3rd person	LI

Appendix A: Diagnostic tests

For a discussion of the purpose of the diagnostic tests, and suggestions for their use, see the Unit 1 Teacher's Manual, p. 102. The words and phrases in **boldface** are either new to students or have occurred infrequently in the reading material up to the Stage indicated.

Test 1

To be given at the end of Stage 16. Translate the title for the students before reading the story aloud to them.

somnium mīrābile

Sextus et Titus erant amīcī. ad urbem **iter faciēbant**. postquam ad urbem pervēnērunt, Sextus ad tabernam contendit. Titus tamen apud frātrem manēbat. post cēnam Titus, quod fessus erat, mox obdormīvit. subitō Sextus in **somniō** appāruit.

"amīce!" inquit. "**caupō** mē necāre vult. necesse est tibi mē **adiuvāre**."

Titus statim surrēxit, quod **commōtus** erat, et sibi dīxit,

"num caupō amīcum meum necāre vult? minimē! somnium erat."

Titus iterum obdormīvit. Sextus iterum in somniō appāruit.

"ēheu!" inquit. "mortuus sum. caupō **scelestus** mē necāvit. postquam mē necāvit, in **plaustrō** mē **cēlāvit**. tū eum pūnīre dēbēs."

Titus ē lectō perterritus surrēxit. ad **vigilēs** festīnāvit remque nārrāvit. tum cum duōbus vigilibus ad tabernam contendit. caupōnem rogāvit,

"ubi est Sextus, amīcus meus, quī in hāc tabernā manēbat?"

"**errōrem** facis," caupō eī respondit. "**nēmō** est in tabernā."

Titus, ubi plaustrum in viā cōnspexit, clāmāvit,

"ecce! amīcus meus, quem tū necāvistī, in hōc plaustrō **cēlātus** est."

vigilēs, postquam plaustrum īnspexērunt, Sextum invēnērunt mortuum. caupōnem attonitum **comprehendērunt**, et eum ad **iūdicem** dūxērunt.

Test 2

To be given at the end of Stage 18, preferably in two successive lessons. Translate the title for the students before reading the Latin aloud.

ad pȳramidas

I

Translate

ōlim Quīntus ad tabernam Clēmentis contendit. ubi ad tabernam pervēnit, Clēmentem salūtāvit.

"salvē, amīce," inquit. "ego tibi aliquid dīcere volō. ad **pȳramidas** iter facere cupiō. sunt enim in Aegyptō multae pȳramides quās Aegyptiī ōlim **exstrūxērunt**. Aegyptiī in pȳramidibus rēgēs **sepelīre** solēbant. ego pȳramidas vidēre volō quod sunt maximae et pulcherrimae. vīsne mēcum iter facere?"

Clēmēns laetus cōnsēnsit. itaque Quīntus et Clēmēns pecūniam cibumque in **saccīs** posuērunt. tum ad Plūtum, mercātōrem Graecum, festīnāvērunt et **camēlōs condūxērunt**. saccōs, quōs ē tabernā Clēmentis portāverant, in camēlīs posuērunt. tum camēlōs **cōnscendērunt** et ex urbe discessērunt. per agrōs et vīllās prōcēdēbant.

subitō decem Aegyptiī, quī **īnsidiās** parāverant, **impetum** fēcērunt. Quīntus et Clēmēns fortiter resistēbant sed facile erat Aegyptiīs eōs superāre quod fūstēs ingentēs habēbant. tum Aegyptiī cum pecūniā et camēlīs effūgērunt. Quīntus et Clēmēns trīstēs ad urbem reveniēbant.

"ēheu!" inquit Clēmēns. "quam miserī sumus! pȳramidas nōn vīdimus: pecūniam et camēlōs āmīsimus."

II

Read the rest of the story and answer the questions at the end.

Quīntus et Clēmēns per urbem fessī prōcēdēbant. ubi tabernam Plūtī **praeterībant**, rem mīrābilem vīdērunt. camēlī, quōs Aegyptiī **abdūxerant**, **extrā** tabernam Plūtī stābant! tum Quīntus rem tōtam intellēxit. amīcī īrātī mercātōrem quaesīvērunt, sed invenīre nōn poterant. aderat tamen puer parvus quī camēlōs custōdiēbat. Quīntus clāmāvit,

"heus, tū! ubi sunt Aegyptiī quī in nōs impetum fēcērunt? ego eōs dē pecūniā meā **interrogāre** volō."

puer perterritus

"rogā Plūtum," inquit, et statim fūgit.

amīcī per viās Alexandrīae Plūtum frūstrā quaesīvērunt. tandem portuī appropinquāvērunt. ecce! Plūtus cum **duōbus** Aegyptiīs negōtium agēbat. Quīntus hominēs agnōvit. eōs enim vīderat in turbā Aegyptiōrum quī impetum fēcerant. Quīntus ad Plūtum prōcessit, quī, postquam eum īrātum vīdit, valdē timēbat.

"ubi est mea pecūnia?" inquit Quīntus. "camēlōs iam invēnimus!"

Plūtus erat perterritus quod Quīntus erat cīvis Rōmānus. Plūtus Quīntō "**ignōsce** mihi," inquit. "decōrum est mihi pecūniam reddere. dōnum quoque tibi offerre volō."

deinde Quīntum et Clēmentem ad vīllam suam dūxit. ibi eīs duōs equōs dedit. Quīntus numquam equōs pulchriōrēs quam illōs vīderat! tum Quīntus et Clēmēns equōs cōnscendērunt et ad pȳramidas laetī contendērunt.

Questions

1 How were Quintus and Clemens feeling when they got back to the city?
2 How did they know they were on the track of the thieves?
3 What question did Quintus ask the boy?
4 What did the boy reply?
5 Where was Plutus and what was he doing when Quintus and Clemens found him?
6 What did Quintus notice about the Egyptian men attending Plutus?
7 Why was Plutus so frightened when Quintus told him about the camels?
8 What happened when Plutus took Quintus and Clemens to his house?
9 What did Quintus think of Plutus' presents?
10 How does the story end?

Answers

1 They were tired.
2 They saw their camels outside Plutus' shop.
3 He asked where the Egyptians were who had attacked him (and Clemens).
4 He said, "Ask Plutus!"
5 Plutus was in the harbor doing business with two Egyptians.
6 The men had been part of the ambush.
7 Quintus was a Roman citizen (and he was not).
8 Plutus gave Quintus and Clemens two horses as presents.
9 He had never seen horses more beautiful than those.
10 Quintus and Clemens rode the horses to visit the pyramids.

Test 3

To be given at the end of Stage 20, preferably in two successive lessons. Translate the title for the students before reading the Latin aloud.

testāmentum Barbillī

I

Translate

multī amīcī cum Galatēā et Aristōne cēnābant. dē morte Barbillī **sermōnem** habēbant.

"magnum **lēgātum** exspectō," inquit Galatēa. "nam ubi Barbillus aeger iacēbat, eum cotīdiē vīsitābam. magnam partem diēī cum eō **cōnsūmēbam**."

omnēs Galatēam laudāvērunt et clāmāvērunt,

"decōrum est tibi praemium accipere."

Petrō, medicus Graecus, triclīnium intrāvit. Galatēa, ubi eum cōnspexit, īrāta surrēxit.

"cūr hūc vēnistī?" inquit. "nos omnēs tē **dēspicimus**, quod tū Barbillum sānāre nōn poterās."

"ego hūc vēnī, quod tibi aliquid dīcere volō," respondit Petrō.

"quid est?" rogāvit Galatēa.

"**testāmentum** Barbillī vīdī," respondit ille.

Galatēa, ubi hoc audīvit, **īram dēposuit**. Petrōnem in mediōs amīcōs dūxit et cibum vīnumque eī obtulit.

"ō **dulcissime**," inquit Galatēa, "quam libenter tē vidēmus. **dīc** nōbīs quam celerrimē dē testāmentō! quid Barbillus nōbīs relīquit?"

II

Read the rest of the story and answer the questions at the end.

omnēs tacuērunt et Petrōnem intentē audīvērunt.

"Barbillus Aristōnī nūllam pecūniam relīquit," inquit Petrō, "sed tragoediās, quās Aristō scrīpsit, reddidit."

amīcī, ubi hoc audīvērunt, valdē rīsērunt quod tragoediae Aristōnis pessimae erant. Galatēa quoque rīsit.

"optimē fēcit Barbillus," inquit Galatēa. "Barbillus Aristōnī tragoediās **sōlum** relīquit quod Aristō nihil aliud cūrat. **sine dubiō** Barbillus mihi multam pecūniam relīquit quod ego sapientior sum quam marītus meus."

tum Petrō Galatēae dīxit.

"Barbillus fīliae tuae **gemmās** pretiōsās, quās ā mercātōre **Syriō** ēmerat, relīquit."

"quam fortūnāta est Helena!" exclāmāvērunt amīcī.

Galatēa hanc rem graviter ferēbat.

"nōn decōrum est Helenae gemmās habēre. nam Helena est stultior quam pater. **tūtius est** Helenae gemmās mihi trādere. sed cūr nihil dē mē dīcis, Petrō? quid Barbillus mihi relīquit?"

Petrō tamen nihil respondit.

Galatēa īrāta

"dīc mihi, stultissime," inquit.

tandem Petrō susurrāvit,

"nihil tibi relīquit."

omnēs amīcī valdē commōtī erant: multī cachinnāvērunt, paucī lacrimāvērunt.

Galatēa tamen tacēbat. **humī** dēciderat exanimāta.

Questions

1 What did Aristo receive in the will?
2 What did Galatea's friends do when they heard what Aristo had received?
3 What, according to Galatea, was Aristo's only interest in life?
4 What did Galatea hope to receive herself?
5 Why did Galatea's friends describe Helena as **fortūnāta**?
6 Why is the Syrian merchant mentioned?
7 What did Galatea think about her daughter's character?
8 What did she think her daughter should do?
9 From Petro's behavior at the end of the story, find two reasons for supposing that he was embarrassed about telling Galatea what she had received.
10 What did Galatea receive?
11 How did most of Galatea's friends show their feelings about this? How did a few of them behave?
12 What effect did the news have on Galatea?

Answers

1 Aristo received back the tragedies which he had written.
2 They laughed.
3 His only interest was in writing tragedies.
4 She hoped to receive a lot of money.
5 Helena received the jewels which Barbillus had bought from a Syrian merchant.
6 Jewels from Syria would presumably be more expensive.
7 She called her more foolish than her father.
8 She thought Helena should give the jewels to her.
9 At first he said nothing and then he whispered the truth.
10 She received nothing.
11 Most laughed; a few cried.
12 She fainted (fell to the ground unconscious).

Appendix B: Select bibliography

A few books are out of print (OP) but are included in case teachers already possess them or can obtain secondhand copies.

General

Adkins, L. & Adkins, R. *A Handbook to Life in Ancient Rome* (Oxford University Press, 1998)

Giardina, A., ed. *The Romans* (University of Chicago Press, 1993) (Essays on such topics as "The Soldier," "The Slave," "The Freedman," "The Merchant," etc.)

Jones, P. & Sidwell, K., eds *The World of Rome* (Cambridge University Press, 1997)

Kamm, A. *The Romans: An Introduction* (Routledge, 1995)

Lewis, N. & Reinhold, M. *Roman Civilization: A Sourcebook. II The Empire* (Columbia University Press, 1990)

Parkin, T. & Pomeroy, A. *Roman Social History: A Sourcebook* (Routledge, 2007)

Scullard, H. *From the Gracchi to Nero* (Routledge, 2011)

Shelton, J. *As the Romans Did: A Sourcebook in Roman Social History* (Oxford University Press, 1997)

Toner, J. *Popular Culture in Ancient Rome* (Polity Press, 2009)

Roman Britain

Allason-Jones, L., ed. *Artefacts in Roman Britain: Their Purpose and Use* (Cambridge University Press, 2011)

Barrett, A. "The Career of Tiberius Claudius Cogidubnus" *Britannia X* (1979), 227–242

Bogaers, J. E. "King Cogidubnus in Chichester: Another Reading of R.I.B. 91" *Britannia X* (1979), 243–254

Cool, H. E. M. *Eating and Drinking in Roman Britain* (Cambridge University Press, 2006)

Cunliffe, B. *Fishbourne Roman Palace* (Tempus Publications, 1998)

Frere, S. S. *Britannia: A History of Roman Britain* (Pimlico Books, 1991)

Henig, M. *Religion in Roman Britain* (Routledge, 2003)

Henig, M. *The Art of Roman Britain* (Routledge, 1995)

Higgins, C. *Under Another Sky* (The Overlook Press, 2013) (A light travelogue on Roman Britain by a journalist with a Classics background.)

Ireland, S. *Roman Britain: A Sourcebook* (Routledge, 2008)

Mattingly, D. *An Imperial Possession: Britain in the Roman Empire* (Penguin, 2007) (Great place to begin research: readable and reliable.)

Millett, M. & Revell, L., eds *The Oxford Handbook of Roman Britain* (Oxford University Press, 2015)

Rankin, D. *Celts and the Classical World* (Routledge, 1996)

Salway, P. *A History of Roman Britain (Oxford History of England Series)* (Oxford University Press, 1997)

Webster, G. *Boudica: The British Revolt against Rome AD 60* (Routledge, 1993)

Egypt and Alexandria

Bowman, A. K. *Egypt after the Pharaohs: 332 BC–AD 642* (University of California Press, 1996)

Canfora, L. *The Vanished Library* (University of California Press, 1990)

Capponi, L. *Roman Egypt (Classical World Series)* (Bristol Classical Press, 2011) (Quick, readable introduction.)

La Riche, W. *Alexandria, the Sunken City* (Weidenfeld & Nicholson, 1996) (OP)

Riggs, C., ed. *The Oxford Handbook of Roman Egypt* (Oxford University Press, 2012) (Great place to begin research.)

Egyptian religion

Clark, R. *Myth and Symbol in Ancient Egypt* (Thames & Hudson, 1991)

Wilkinson, R. H. *The Complete Gods and Goddesses of Ancient Egypt* (Thames & Hudson, 2003)

Witt, R. E. *Isis in the Ancient World* (Johns Hopkins University Press, 1997)

Medicine, science, and technology

Bayley, J., Freestone, I., & Jackson, C., eds *Glass of the Roman World* (Oxbow Books, 2015)

Hill, D. A. *History of Engineering in Classical and Medieval Times* (Routledge, 1996)

King, H. *Greek and Roman Medicine (Classical World Series)* (Bristol Classical Press, 2001) (Quick, readable introduction.)

Lee, D. "Science, Philosophy, and Technology in the Greco-Roman World," *Greece and Rome* (1973) 65–78, 180–193

Nunn, J. F. *Ancient Egyptian Medicine* (University of Oklahoma Press, 1996)

Nutton, V. *Ancient Medicine (Sciences of Antiquities Series)* (Routledge, 2012)

Oleson, J. P., ed. *The Oxford Handbook of Engineering and Technology in the Classical World* (Oxford University Press, 2009)

For students

Grant, M. *Routledge Atlas of Classical History* (Routledge, 1994)

McEvedy, C. *Penguin Atlas of Ancient History* (Penguin, 2002)

Roman Britain

Johnston, D., ed. *Discovering Roman Britain* (Shire Publications, 2002)

Martell, H. M. *The Celts* (Cherrytree Books, 2016)

Sealey, P. R. *The Boudican Revolt against Rome* (Shire Publications, 2004)

Wilcox, P. *Rome's Enemies: Gallic and British Celts* (Osprey, 1986)

Egypt

Dodsworth, R. *Glass and Glassmaking* (Shire Publications, 1982)

Ellis, S. P. *Graeco-Roman Egypt* (Shire Publications, 1992)

Forster, E. M. *Alexandria: A History and Guide* (Tauris Parke, 2014)

Hart, G. *Ancient Egypt* (Dorling Kindersley, 2014)

Putnam, J. *An Introduction to Egyptology* (Chartwell, 2002)

Walker, S. & Bierbrier, M. *Ancient Faces: Mummy Portraits from Roman Egypt* (Routledge, 2000)

Historical novels

Bradshaw, G. *The Beacon at Alexandria* (Houghton Mifflin, 1986) (A young woman escapes an arranged marriage to study medicine in Alexandria in the fourth century.)

Davis, L. *The Silver Pigs* (Minotaur Books, 2011) (The first in a series of adventures of the Roman detective Falco. The fourteenth book, *The Jupiter Myth*, is set in Roman Britain and the nineteenth, *Alexandria*, in Roman Egypt.)

Duggan, A. *The Little Emperors* (Bello, 2012) (About a series of coups in Roman Britain.)

Evans, I. *Gadget City: A Story of Ancient Alexandria* (Frederick Warne, 1951) (A Welsh slave captured in Britain is sent to work at the Museum in Alexandria.) (OP)

Lawrence, C. *Escape from Rome* (Orion Children's Books, 2016) (The first in the new *Roman Quests* series of adventure stories for children set in Roman Britain during the reign of Domitian.)

Lawrence, C. *The Thieves of Ostia* (Orion Children's Books, 2002) (*The Roman Mysteries* series follows the adventures of four children who solve mysteries. Books XIV and XV, *The Beggar of Volubilis* and *The Scribes from Alexandria*, are set in North Africa and Alexandria.)

Sutcliff, R. *The Eagle (The Roman Britain Trilogy)* (Square Fish, 2011) (The first book in the trilogy has been made into a movie of the same name.)

Sutcliff, R. *Outcast* (Farrar, Straus and Giroux, 1995) (A shipwrecked Roman infant grows up with a British tribe.)

Treece, H. *Legions of the Eagle* (Bodley Head, 1972) (The story of a boy living during the invasion of AD 43.) (OP)

Treece, H. *War Dog* (Criterion Books, 1963) (A story about Bran, the huge war dog of Caratacus' charioteer.) (OP)